THE PINK HOUSE

THE PINK HOUSE:

THE LEGENDARY RESIDENCE OF EDWIN BRADFORD HALL AND HIS SUCCEEDING GENERATIONS IN WELLSVILLE, NEW YORK

William A. Paquette, Ph.D.
Professor of History

Julian B. Woelfel, D.D.S.

Marcile B. Woelfel

NEW DOMINION PRESS

New Dominion Press • Norfolk • Virginia

The Pink House:
The Legendary Residence of Edwin Bradford Hall, and His Succeeding Generations in Wellsville, New York

Published by:

New Dominion Press

New Dominion Media/New Dominion Press
1217 Godfrey Avenue, Norfolk, Virginia 23504-3218
www.NewDominionPress.com

First Printing: October 2018

Cover design, Graphics Design, and Typography by New Dominion Press

Publisher's Cataloging-in-Publication Data
provided by Five Rainbows Cataloging Services

Names: Paquette, William A., 1947- author. | Woelfel, Julian B., author. | Woelfel, Marcille B., author.
Title: The pink house: the legendary residence of Edwin Bradford Hall and his succeeding generations in
    Wellsville, New York / William A. Paquette, Julian B. Woelfel, [and] Marcille B. Woelfel.
Description: Norfolk, VA : New Dominion Press, 2018. | Includes bibliographical references and index.
Identifiers: LCCN 2018951360 | ISBN 978-0-692-18359-5 (hardcover) | ISBN 978-1-7357483-2-0 (pbk.)
Subjects: LCSH: Hall family. | Farnum family. | Families--History. | Historic buildings--New York (State) |
    New York (State)--History. | Biography. | BISAC: HISTORY / United States / State & Local / Middle
    Atlantic (DC, DE, MD, NJ, NY, PA) | HISTORY / Modern / General. | BIOGRAPHY &
    AUTOBIOGRAPHY / General.
Classification: LCC CS69 .P37 2018 (print) | LCC CS69 (ebook) | DDC 929.209747/84--dc23.

First Edition

Dedication

Edwin Bradford Hall
(1825-1908)
Governor William Bradford descendant.
Bridgeport, Connecticut native.
Wellsville, New York resident.

A man who came with dreams and ideas; a love for family and community, and left for posterity a legendary drug store, a museum ready fossil collection, and a fabled residence.

Table of Contents

THE PINK HOUSE - ADDED TO TWO HISTORIC REGISTERS
The New York State & National Registers of Historic Places

In the Fall of 2019, Mrs. Marcile Woelfel, the owner of *The Pink House*, decided it was time to place Edwin Bradford Hall's legendary residence on the National Register of Historic Places. A listing on the National Register is a two-step process. The structure must first be approved by the State Historic Registry where the building is located. This first step is quite complicated because of the details, which must be provided about the residence's history, construction, and why the building deserves an historic designation. Once approved by the home State and added to a State Registry, the application is forwarded to the Department of the Interior for review as a National Historic Place. The key to securing Historic Status for *The Pink House* was finding a person in Allegany County, New York who could establish contact with the New York State Register of Historic Sites and conduct the research.

That person was found: Ron Taylor, the Executive Director of The Allegany County Historical Society and Museum. With Mrs. Woelfel's support and the promise of my assistance as the author of *The Pink House...,* the process began in late 2019. The research, documentation, and photographic requirements took Ron Taylor and me nine months to complete. His hard work was rewarded with helpful assistance from a board member on the New York State Board for Historic Preservation. Unfortunately, before the completed application could be submitted, Marcile Woelfel passed away August 3, 2020. Ron and I had her blessing, and we remained confident that the application would be finished and accepted.

The New York State Board unanimously approved *The Pink House* application and Governor Andrew Cuomo announced September 14, 2021 that *The Pink House* was added to the State and National Register of Historic Places. Governor Cuomo said "… By placing these landmarks on the State and National Registers of Historic Places, we are helping to ensure these places and their caretakers have the funding needed to preserve, improve, and promote the best of this great state.

The Pink House, Wellsville, Allegany County- built in 1866, this Italianate-style villa also includes intact historic period features including marble statuary, an ice-house, a three-story carriage barn, a gazebo, and a building known as the Fossil House, where original owner Edwin B. Hall stored his extensive fossil collection that now resides at the New York State Museum in Albany and the Carnegie Museum in Pittsburgh. Still in family ownership, the home retains its original pink exterior color that gives it its name."

On March 4, 2021, *The Pink House* was accepted for the National Historic Register of Historic Places. The extensive interior and exterior restorations undertaken by the late Dr. Julian and late Marcile Woelfel over a thirty-year period were rewarded by the residence's acceptance on the New York State and National Historic Registries. *The Pink House* remains a family residence with the baton of ownership passing to the fifth generation to Jay, Julian and Marcile's youngest son, and his wife, Kristy.

William A. Paquette, Ph.D.
August 3, 2021

INTRODUCTION

The publication of *The Pink House* was made possible with the cooperation of its owners, Dr. Julian and Marcile B. Woelfel of Dublin, Ohio. Our journey together began in 2014, when I contacted Julian and Marcile and shared with them a copy of an article I published in the *Humanities Review* about Governor William Bradford, Edwin Bradford Hall, and *The Pink House*. As Past Governor of the Virginia Mayflower Society and a professional historian, I encouraged them to let me assist in proving their line of descent from Governor William Bradford. A four-year adventure began in successfully documenting Julian's ancestry to Governor William Bradford enabling him to join the General Society of Mayflower Descendants in 2016 and encouraging them to publish a pictorial history on *The Pink House*, which led to a special friendship with two very generous and extraordinary people.

I was fortunate to attend my junior and senior high school years at Wellsville High School in Wellsville, New York. One block away was the legendary residence of Edwin Bradford Hall, *The Pink House*. My fascination with 19th century history was manifested in higher education degrees in history and a college career of teaching and publication. The history of *The Pink House* is unique because it is one of the few Victorian-era residences to remain in the possession of the same family for four generations. Victorian residences are 19th century fantasies created as monuments to their original owner's financial success and their personal tastes and interests. Each residence is an exuberant expression of achieving the American financial dream, the love of family and faith, and the opportunity to explore avocations during an era in United States History when the country was rapidly becoming an urban and industrial nation. Economic success enabled Americans to cast off the simple and austere architecture of houses that were two rooms over two. Multi-storied residences, many with towers and multiple wings, permitted larger and more rooms with specialized functions. The interiors celebrated the latest in technological innovation in plumbing, lighting, and heating. The decorative arts were given full expression in the beautifully carved woodwork that celebrated the varieties of local hard and soft woods and the skills of local immigrant artisans. Victorian homes were dedicated to more than the customary cooking, eating, and sleeping functions. Victorian homes permitted family members to experience beauty and comfort while developing their own talents and skills. But, it was not only the exterior and interior that Victorian houses celebrated. These residences celebrated the landscaped grounds and decorative gardens, which enhanced the beauty of the architecture in their midst. Landscaped grounds with fountains and ornamentals were gathering places for family and friends to celebrate birthdays, christenings, weddings, funerals, and the seasons of spring, summer, fall, and winter. Victorians were social. Both the gardens and grounds along with the residential interiors brought family and friends frequently together to appreciate special moments.

The Pink House has always been a private residence. It has never been open to the public. Therefore, this may be the reason for the many unexplained stories that surfaced over 150 years about the home built by Edwin Bradford Hall. Mr. Hall and his descendants remained very private people in both the celebration of life and the sadness of grief over death. Mrs. Fannie Hall Carpenter, the daughter of Edwin B. Hall, lived a more secluded life after the death of her husband, John Milton Carpenter, in 1926 until her own death in 1958. As a result, the house retreated more from the realm of social interaction. Mrs. Carpenter's daughter, Florence Carpenter Woelfel, lived permanently in Columbus, Ohio returning to Wellsville for a few months each year. It was not until the retirement of Dr. Julian Woelfel in 1995, Edwin B. Hall's great-grandson, that *The Pink House* once again came back to life and was reintegrated into the Wellsville community under Julian's and Marcile's stewardship.

On behalf of Dr. Julian and Marcile Woelfel I invite you to *The Pink House*. This is a ghost free tour. *The Pink House* never had ghosts. Mary Frances Farnum never haunted *The Pink House* because it never existed during her short life time. The death of two-year old Beatrice Carpenter was a private family tragedy. As you page through the story of *The Pink House* enjoy the travel back in time to Wellsville's early days. Rediscover the accomplishments of Edwin Bradford Hall as a successful druggist, a gifted amateur fossil collector, and talented architect. Rediscover the roles played by Antoinette Farnum Hall, her daughter Fannie Hall Carpenter, and Mrs. Hall's sister, Louise Farnum Brown, in the establishment of Wellsville's David A. Howe Public Library. My only regret is that Dr. Julian Woelfel died unexpectedly on September 2, 2017 and could not be with us to celebrate the publication of *The Pink House* but he remains with us in spirit.

William A. Paquette, Ph.D.
Professor of History

CHAPTER ONE

The Farnum Family

Allegany County New York was created in 1806 from the original Holland Land Purchase. The County's borders were defined by 1857 after land was ceded to neighboring Steuben, Cattaraugus, Wyoming, and Livingston Counties. The Seneca Indians were forced to cede their land claims prior to the American Revolution and European settlement did not begin until after the United States achieved its independence.

19th century drawing showing the Farnum house near the mill run and the Pink House one block above on the upper left side of the map

Edward Judson Farnum as a young man

Lucy Goff Farnum and daughter Louise Farnum, 1860s, and before Louise's marriage to Alfred Brown

New Englanders started to migrate west after the Revolution given land scarcity for farming to accommodate new generations of the region's large families. The sale of land at a cheap price in the former Holland Land Purchase enticed many a New Englander into Western New York. Allegany County's southern border is the Pennsylvania state line. The County is divided into two almost equal parts by the Genesee River, which flows north to Lake Ontario from Pennsylvania. The decision by the Erie Railroad to build track across the Southern Tier of New York brought railroad civil engineer Edward Judson Farnum to Wellsville, New York in 1847.

Edward Judson Farnum was born in Uxbridge, Massachusetts on March 16, 1809. His parents were Caleb Farnum and Sylvania Allen. He was one of ten children, four brothers and five sisters; two of whom died in infancy. His father was a factory superintendent in Slatersville, Rhode Island; Jewett City, Connecticut; and Rochester, New York. Edward Farnum gained employment in each one of the factories his father supervised. While employed in Rochester, New York, E. J. Farnum met his first wife, Lucy Goff. They were married in February 1829 by the Reverend Asa Mahan in nearby Pittsford. The newlyweds moved to Bath, New York where his father, Caleb Farnum, had purchased a farm. In Steuben County Farnum studied to become a civil engineer while working as a clerk and a teacher.

From 1837 to 1838, Edward Farnum worked for the Buffalo and Mississippi Railroad as a resident engineer in Indiana and in 1838 was hired by the Erie Railroad. He purchased a farm in Bath, which his wife managed when he was away. His survey work for the intended Erie Railroad route through Wellsville, convinced Farnum that the dense pine forests of Allegany County, offered significant investment

Residence of Hon. EDWARD J. FARNUM, State Street, WELLSVILLE, N. Y.

1879 drawing of the Farnum residence on West State Street, one block south of the Pink House

opportunities. Wellsville in the 1840s was an emerging community straddling the Genesee River and home to lumber mills and tanneries. Farnum believed his financial future could be secured by settling in Wellsville. He brought his family to Wellsville in 1847, giving him a four-year window of opportunity to invest before the first trains arrived in 1851.

All seven of Edward and Lucy Farnum's children were born in Bath. Two died in infancy and were buried in Bath, Sarah Farnum, born March 4, 1835, died March 19, 1835 and Edward Fayette Farnum born February 4, 1838, died August 21, 1841. His surviving five children were Antoinette, born 1832 (day and month never recorded), Mary Frances, born December 31, 1835, William Carlton, born January 10, 1840, Louise Adelaide, born September 6, 1842, and Sylvania, born August 2, 1846. E. J. Farnum built a home for his family on West State Street on one side of the Genesee River with his farm further down on the opposite river bank.

Edward Farnum acquired over three-thousand acres of land in Wellsville, which originally included what is now Woodlawn Cemetery and Island Park, and established his lumber business. Farnum's parents and siblings followed him to Wellsville. E. J. Farnum felled the trees and processed the timber at his sawmills while his brother, Carleton Lee Farnum, became a building contractor. Contemporary biographies of Mr. Farnum describe him as a

William Carlton Farnum, son of E. J. and Lucy Goff Farnum

Sylvania Farnum, youngest daughter of E. J. and Lucy Farnum, crippled by polio

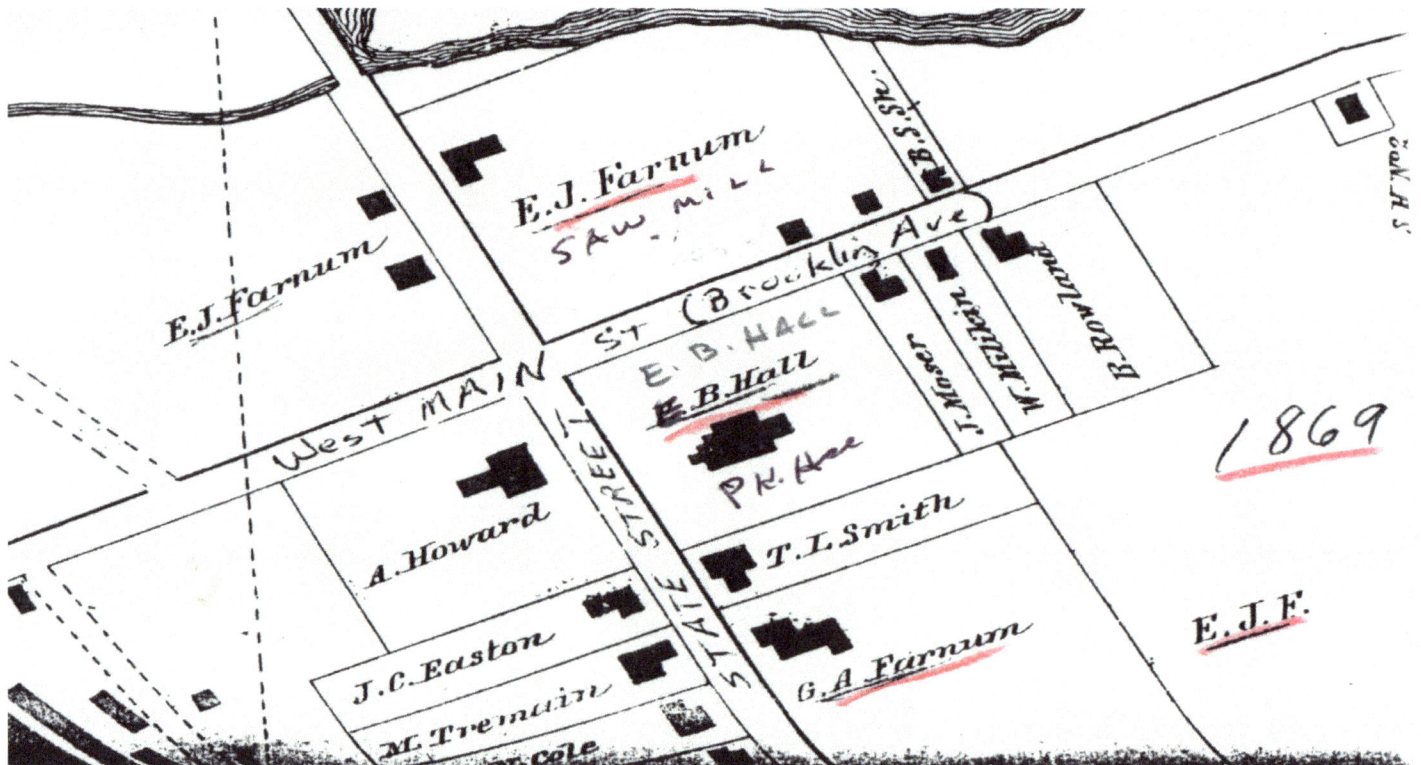

Beers Insurance Map showing relationship of Farnum and Hall properties

8

E. J. Farnum's Constitutional Convention Chair, 1867-68, donated to the New York State Museum in Albany

Reverend F. W. Beecher, minister First Congregational Church, Wellsville and nephew of Uncle Tom's Cabin author Harriet Beecher Stowe.

man of integrity, having an indomitable will and perseverance, and refusing the notion of failure. Lumberman E. J. Farnum was also a lover of nature and he was responsible for the planting of over two thousand shade trees in Wellsville along Main Street, State Street, and the highways entering Wellsville. His popularity and modesty were rewarded with his selection to be a delegate for the 30th District, Allegany County at the State Constitutional Convention from 1867-68. His delegate chair/desk was kept by his Hall descendants until recently when it was donated to the Albany State Library of New York.

Edward Farnum was President of the Wellsville's First National Bank and at the time of his death was the bank's vice-president and director. The Farnum family were members of the First Congregational Church. Mr. Farnum was a member of the committee charged in

1871 with finding a new site for the Church. The location chosen on North Main Street was coincidentally next door to the residence of his daughter, Louise Farnum Brown. The new church was dedicated on March 12, 1874 by Reverend Thomas K. Beecher, a brother of author Harriet Beecher Stowe. His nephew, Reverend Frederick W. Beecher became the pastor for Wellsville's First Congregational Church on March 15, 1874 and remained as the Church's minister until June 26, 1892. The Farnum and Beecher families remained in close contact for decades.

Lucy Goff Farnum was a quiet and sustaining presence to her husband and children. She successfully managed the family farm and participated when needed in her husband's other business interests while he worked as a civil engineer. A contemporary of Lucy Farnum (Mrs. Mary White) described her as the best woman

First Congregational Church, built in 1874

Farnum house under Harder ownership showing alterations to the original structure

The Late Hon. EDWARD J. FARNUM,
of Wellsville, N. Y.

E. J. Farnum in Old Age

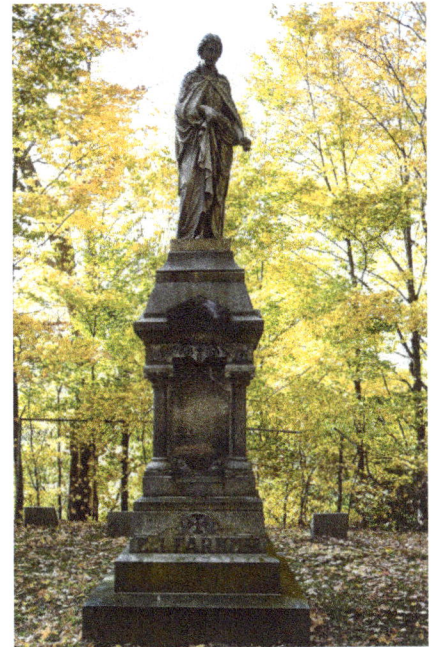

Farnum burial plot, Woodlawn Cemetery

E. J. Farnum Grave, Woodlawn Cemetery

she ever knew, who took food baskets to less fortunate families, and who was a member of the Congregational Church. Her death on October 12, 1876 was a severe blow to E. J. Farnum, his family, and to those in Wellsville on whom she bestowed her help and support. After Lucy's death, E. J. Farnum began to go astray and his daughters, Antoinette and Louise, approached Miss Loretta Wildman to encourage her to marry their father with a $10,000 incentive. A tall, severe looking woman in her mid-forties who had never married, Lettie was described as nice with good ancestry. Edward Farnum and Lettie Wildman were wed on June 30th, 1881, and the marriage proved beneficial to both.

Edward Judson Farnum died on July 11, 1894 at the age of 85. He seemed in good health just returning home with his wife from a business trip to neighboring Potter County in Pennsylvania. He became suddenly ill and passed away quietly; his heart gave out. His funeral was one of the largest ever held in Wellsville. All Wellsville businesses were closed on the day of the funeral to honor Mr. Farnum. The service was held at the Congregational Church with burial on the former Farnum farm, then known as the Farnum Cemetery; later renamed Woodlawn Cemetery.

Edward Farnum's will left special bequests to his invalid daughter, Sylvania, and his two grandchildren Fannie Hall and Edward Brown. The rest of the estate was divided into five parts with his widow, Lettie, and each one of his four surviving children inheriting one-fifth of the estate. Mrs. Farnum was given life use of their Mountain View farm.

His son, William Carlton never married and moved to a residence on Brooklyn Avenue. He was a successful businessman with interests in lumber, milling, and farming, which he pursued until ill health forced him to retire. As a young man, he was engaged in lumber interests in Patterson, New Jersey and Three Rivers, Canada, but eventually returned to Wellsville. W. C. was known as a man of courtesy, kindness, and concentration and one who maintained friendships, once established, his entire life. He was a charitable, generous, and obliging resident who lived a simple life and was a familiar face around the community. William Carlton Farnum was never married, died February 7, 1913 and left an estate valued at over $53,000 to his surviving sisters, Antoinette Hall and Louise Brown. William Carleton Farnum was buried in the Farnum plot with his parents and sisters Mary Frances Farnum and Sylvania Farnum.

Sylvania Farnum was bedridden most of her life. She was crippled by polio and confined to either a wheel chair or to bed. After her mother's death, she alternated living with her sisters, Antoinette Hall and Louise Farnum. At the Pink House, she lived on the first floor in a suite of rooms next to the breakfast room and near an exterior door to an outside walkway (now gone) connecting the main house to the Ice House. Sylvania was regarded as a kind and intelligent young lady who bore her illness with great fortitude and without complaint. She died August 12, 1904 and was buried in the Farnum lot. The second Mrs. E. J. Farnum died January 27, 1916 and is buried with her parents in Woodlawn Cemetery.

Loretta Wildman Farnum, second wife of E. J. Farnum, grave with the Wildman family, Woodlawn Cemetery

The Farnum residence on West State Street was sold to the Harder family and during the 20th century had several sections detached creating separate homes with the main structure divided into four apartments.

Farnum house, 2017, greatly altered side view with the front facing West State Street

To commemorate their parents lives and contributions to Wellsville, Antoinette Farnum Hall and Louise Farnum Brown contributed the money to purchase a magnificent stained-glass window of *Christ in the Garden of Gethsemane* made in Rochester, New York for the First Congregational Church. When the First Congregational Church was torn down in 1968, the Farnum window was the only stained-glass window saved and installed in the new First Congregational Church at 289 North Main Street.

Current First Congregational Church with Farnum window in front

Exterior view of the Farnum window, First Congregational Church

Interior view of the Farnum window, First Congregational Church

CHAPTER TWO

Edwin Bradford Hall

Edwin Bradford Hall was born on October 25, 1825 in Fairfield, Connecticut, the eldest of two sons of Ebenezer (Eben) Hoyt Hall and Mary Ann Bradford, a direct descendant of Pilgrim Governor William Bradford. This line of descent was very important to the Hall family and is noted in the biographical essays written about them. Being a Pilgrim descendant indicated exceptional character and strong moral and religious values.

A young Edwin Bradford Hall, 1860s tintype frame

Eben Hoyt Hall, Edwin Hall's father

Mary Ann Bradford Hall, Edwin B. and Albert Hall's mother

Edwin Hall was an eighth-generation descendant of Governor Bradford: Governor William Bradford (gen. 1); Major William Bradford (gen. 2); Lieutenant Joseph Bradford (gen. 3); Joseph Bradford (gen. 4), Henry Swift Bradford (gen. 5), Silas Bradford (gen. 6), Mary Ann Bradford Hall (gen. 7). This Bradford line of descent was verified and Dr. Julian Woelfel became a member of the General Society of Mayflower Descendants and the Mayflower State Societies in Virginia and Ohio in 2016. Hall's Bradford line of descent left Massachusetts Bay Colony in the late 17th century. They moved to Connecticut settling in Bridgeport in Fairfield County. In the late 18th century Henry Swift Bradford and his son Silas Bradford moved to Blenheim, New York in Schoharie County as land opened for farming. Mary Ann Bradford was probably born in Blenheim, but her family kept in touch with relatives in Fairfield County (Connecticut) bringing her into contact with Ebenezer Hoyt Hall. Eben Hall and Mary Ann Bradford were married in Blenheim (New York) in 1820 and settled back in Bridgeport, Connecticut.

The Hall family was descended from Francis Hall, a resident of Kent in England who moved to New Haven in Connecticut in the mid-17th century. Francis Hall purchased land in Fairfield County, Connecticut in 1654 and 1659 where he was a practicing attorney. Francis Hall's eldest son, Isaac Hall, practiced medicine in Fairfield County. Each generation of Halls remained in Fairfield County believing the area held economic opportunity. The Hall line of descent was Francis Hall (gen 1), Isaac Hall (gen. 2), Samuel Hall (gen.

*Edwin Bradford Hall 1870s
with beard*

*P. T. Barnum, a resident of Bridgeport, Connecticut,
the hometown of E. B. Hall*

3), Isaac Hall II (gen. 4), Samuel Hall (gen. 5), Ebenezer Hall (gen. 6), and Ebenezer Hall (gen. 7). Eben Hall, Edwin Bradford Hall's father, was a grocer in Bridgeport. Both Edwin Hall and his younger brother, John Albert Hall, worked in the family business. The family home was north of the city center of Bridgeport in an area of small homes housing Irish and German immigrants. There were two substantial residences in this neighborhood, the home of General Tom Thumb of P. T. Barnum fame and the Eli Thompson house, which appears to be a mirror image of the Pink House, and which was torn down in the 1890s. The grocery business was apparently a struggle because Eben Hall kept remortgaging the family home. The Hall financial difficulties are confirmed in the will of Silas Bradford, Eben's father-in-law, who left his daughter and son-in-

law a sum of money provided Eben had repaid the monies borrowed. Both the Hall residence and the grocery store were razed during later periods of Bridgeport redevelopment.

Edwin Bradford Hall left Bridgeport after he was certified as a pharmacist, and he joined his mother's younger brother, Clark Bradford, in establishing a drug store business in Wellsville, New York in 1852. Clark Bradford had been residing in neighboring Steuben County prior to the move to Wellsville. Within a year (1853) Hall purchased his uncle's share of the business. He made the drug store a financial success; securing his family's financial future. Edward Bradford Hall had an exceptional intellect reflected in the success of his business and architectural and avocation interests.

Edwin Bradford Hall in later years

Antoinette Farnum Hall 1860s

Fannie Hall as a young woman

E. B. Hall standing with daughter Fannie Hall Carpenter, and granddaughter Florence Carpenter (Woelfel) standing on wicker chair

Bridgeport, Connecticut was not only home to Edwin Bradford Hall, but it was the home of P. T. Barnum. Barnum is probably best known for the creation of a circus, but Barnum was a unique entrepreneur who found multiple ways to advance his business interests through creative advertising. Perhaps, Hall was aware of some of Barnum's methods and adapted them to his own business enterprises. Given that the Pink House design was so similar to the Bridgeport, Connecticut residence of Eli Thompson, an associate of P. T. Barnum, the suggestion of a Barnum influence in Edwin Hall's business promotions, has merit.

Within a few short years Edwin Bradford Hall was a successful Wellsville businessman and family documents indicate that he had a romantic interest in Mary Frances Farnum, a younger sister of his future wife, Antoinette. Three years after the death of Mary Frances Farnum, Edwin Hall married her older sister, Antoinette. The marriage of E. B. Hall and Antoinette Farnum was a happy one and both delighted in the birth of their daughter, Fannie.

Edwin Bradford Hall, daughter Fannie Hall Carpenter, and granddaughter, Florence Carpenter (Woelfel), 1900

Edwin Bradford Hall and family on front porch of the Pink House with baby Florence

John Albert Hall, Edwin Hall's brother, 1860s

Mary Jane Philan Hall, wife of Albert Hall, E. B. Hall's brother

John Albert Hall, Edwin Hall's younger brother, was born in Bridgeport on May 29, 1829. He, too, worked at the family grocery store, but John, also, became a skilled carpenter. John Albert Hall served in Company I, Twelfth Connecticut Volunteer Infantry during the Civil War serving with General Benjamin Butler at New Orleans and under General Sheridan at the battles of Winchester and Cedar Creek in Virginia. John Albert Hall was captured at Natchez in Mississippi, and imprisoned for three months before parole. Prior to his enlistment, John Hall married Mary Jane Phelan, a former Bridgeport resident, in Poughkeepsie, New York.

They returned to Bridgeport, but after the Civil War, the John Albert Hall family left Connecticut in the winter of 1867-68. John Albert Hall and his family settled in Kansas City, Missouri, where like his brother, Edwin, he became a successful businessman and built an impressive Victorian residence. The two brothers each had one daughter, were Republicans, and attended the Congregational Church. John Albert Hall died March 8, 1915 in Kansas City. The two brothers were in regular contact by mail and the two families continued these communications over several generations.

L to R: Albert Hall, E. B. Hall's younger brother, Edwin Bradford Hall, and an unidentified friend of Mr. Hall's taken in the 1850s

John Albert Hall in later years in Kansas City, Missouri

L to R; E. J. Farnum in the middle with wife Antoinette and a friend on the Pink House grounds

Antoinette Hall seated with a book

Antoinette Hall in later years

E. B. Hall in later years

Edwin Hall returned to Bridgeport several times to attend the funerals of his parents and after both died, returned a final time to erect new headstones for each parent's grave in Mountain Grove Cemetery. Bridgeport's Mountain Grove Cemetery is where P. T. Barnum, General Tom Thumb, and Eli Thompson are also buried.

Each chapter in this book offers information about Edwin Bradford Hall and his family. Together, the chapters reveal a man of great intellect, integrity, and civic mindedness. Sadly, Edwin Hall witnessed the tragic death of his granddaughter, Beatrice Carpenter, who drowned in the fountain that once graced the center of the circular driveway of the Pink House. It was believed that he suffered from conditions related to his heart and/or a possible stroke. Dr. Julian Woelfel, his great-grandson,

believed Edwin Hall may have had Parkinson's Disease. When E. B. Hall died on September 11, 1908, he was approaching his 83rd birthday. His widow, Antoinette Farnum Hall died June 29, 1917. Their funerals were held in the Pink House's double parlors. Edwin and Antoinette Hall are buried together in the Hall-Carpenter-Woelfel mausoleum in Wellsville's Woodlawn Cemetery. Edwin and Antoinette were a modest and retiring couple who quietly supported civic and patriotic causes in Wellsville. Their deaths left a great void in the soul of their community of residence.

Eben Hoyt Hall grave Mountain Grove Cemetery, Bridgeport, CT

Mary Ann Bradford Hall grave Mountain Grove Cemetery, Bridgeport, CT

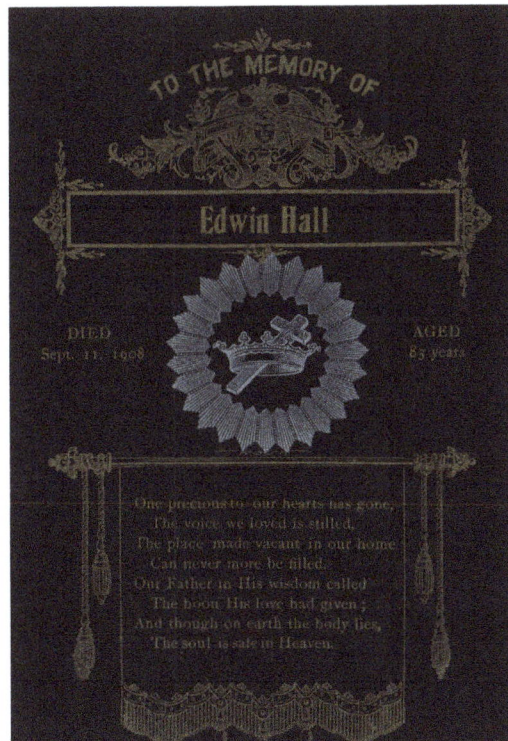

Death card, Edwin Bradford Hall

The Pink House serves as a memorial to their love for each other and to the community which they treasured.

Mr. and Mrs. Hall on the porch and Fannie Hall at the fountain

Antoinette Hall, seated, and Fannie Hall at the Pink House gazebo while playing croquet

Fannie Louise Hall with her mother, Antoinette, in Pink House gardens in 1892

Fannie Louise Hall Carpenter

CHAPTER THREE

Mary Francis Farnum

Much has been written about Frances Farnum, although little can be documented about her life. Most of what has been written about Frances Farnum concerns the circumstances of her death rather than the details of her life.

The pages of a family Bible record the birth of Mary Frances Farnum in Bath, Steuben County New York on December 31, 1835. She was the third daughter of Edward Judson Farnum and Lucy Goff in a family that once numbered seven children. Frances was named for her paternal aunt, Mary Frances Farnum Stoddard.

Daguerreotype image of Frances Farnum as a young woman, 1850s

Portrait of Frances Farnum hanging in the double parlors of the Pink House

In 1847 Frances moved to Wellsville, New York in neighboring Allegany County with her parents and surviving siblings Antoinette, Louise, Sylvania, and William Carleton. A surviving daguerreotype image of Frances Farnum reveals an attractive young woman. It is believed that the portrait of Frances hanging in the double parlors of the *Pink House* was based on this photograph and was painted after her death. On December 14, 1857, Frances died from suicidal drowning in the mill race beside her father's house at 143 West State Street. She was 21 years, 11 months, and 14 days old. Frances is buried in the Farnum plot in Wellsville's Woodlawn Cemetery.

Frances Farnum (1835-1857) grave, Woodlawn Cemetery

Hanford Lennox Gordon (1836-1920)

Her name and memory did not rest in peace. Over two centuries of stories surfaced about forbidden love, fatherly betrayal, and a love triangle. It is impossible to document when these rumors started or who was responsible for them. This author believes the rash of unfounded tales began after Frances' 1857 newspaper obituary, continued with the publication of Hanford Lennox Gordon's poem *Pauline* in 1878, and revived and intensified after the tragic death of Frances Farnum's great-niece, Beatrice Carpenter, by accidental drowning in 1907.

Growing up in Wellsville, Frances Farnum was most likely educated at a local common school where she probably met a student one-year younger than her, the future poet Hanford Lennox Gordon. The family supports the belief that Frances and Hanford became friends. Hanford Lennox Gordon, a man given to adventures and challenges, displayed strong will and determinations to become rich and famous and may have presented himself as quite

a dashing figure. His father was a lumberman as was Frances' father; therefore, the two families knew each other. The elder Mr. Gordon suffered severe financial reversals by 1852, left his wife behind in Wellsville, and moved to Jefferson County, Pennsylvania to rebuild his lumber business; the same year Hanford went to Delhi, New York to study law with an uncle. Hanford Lennox Gordon's mother died in 1854 bringing him back to Wellsville for her burial in Johnson Cemetery. The family of Frances Farnum knew that she and Hanford corresponded while he studied the law and the two may have seen each other when he attended his mother's funeral.

The correspondence between Frances and Hanford ended about the time Frances and Edwin Bradford Hall, a successful Wellsville druggist ten years older than she, started to exchange communications. None of the correspondence between Frances Farnum and Hanford Lennox Gordon survives. But, there are surviving communications between Edwin Hall and

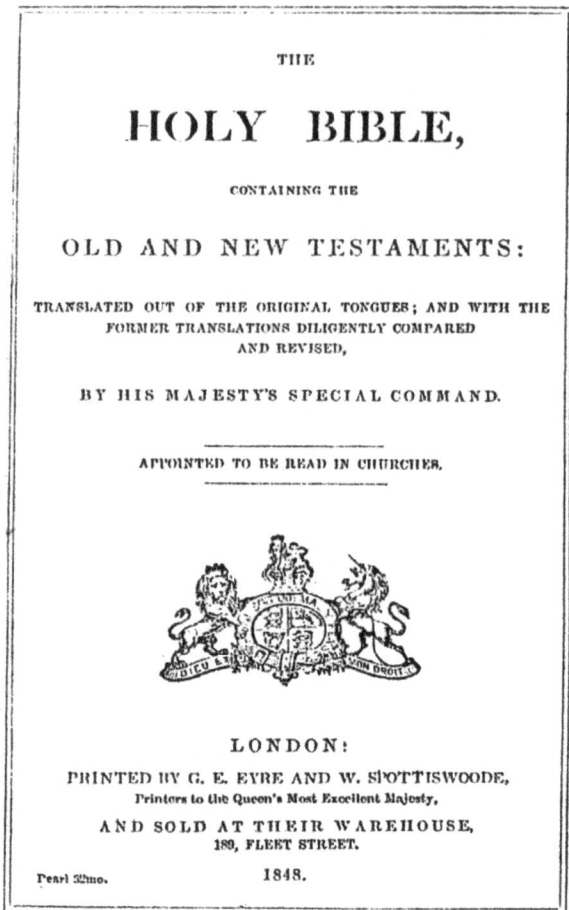

Bible title page with inscription as Philopena by Frances Farnum to E. B. Hall

Frances Farnum that include two poems written by Mr. Hall to Frances for Valentine's Day 1856 and 1857, an undated communication from Edwin Hall to Frances suggesting a meeting at her uncle, George Farnum's, house, and a Bible inscribed *Philopena* from Frances Farnum to Edwin Hall.

The term *Philopena* refers to a game of German origin when a person finds a double kernelled almond or nut offers the second kernel to another person demanding a forfeit at their next meeting. The forfeit could be a simple greeting exchange or something more elaborate. *Philopena* was considered a game of flirtation discussed much later in Louisa May Alcott's *An Old-Fashioned Girl* (1870). To practice *Philopena*

was considered an indelicate practice for a well-bred young lady.

Within the Farnum family it was known that Mr. Farnum intercepted letters from Hanford Lennox Gordon to his daughter Frances. It is possible that Edward Farnum was more comfortable with his daughter developing a relationship with Mr. Hall, an older successful businessman than with a sometimes brash and abrasive younger man who had yet to establish himself in a career and who might never return to Wellsville given his frequent travels while studying the law. It was not uncommon in the 19th century for older men, once successful, to marry younger women with the encouragement of the young woman's father.

In 1857 Hanford Lennox Gordon did return to Wellsville and opened a law practice in neighboring Scio only to fall into heavy debt because of a financial crash that same year.

What triggered Frances Farnum's suicide on December 14, 1857, will never be known. The newspaper obituary printed in the *Hornellsville Tribune* three days later states that Frances Farnum in a "...fit of melancholy, and partial derangement, induced by an unnatural state of religious excitement, stealthy left her room in her father's house, and repairing to the mill race nearby, threw herself into the water..." Frances Farnum was described as a young lady of superior moral worth and loveliness but subject to fits of melancholy and fears that she may have committed an unpardonable sin.

What we know is that Frances' robe and shoes were found on the bridge where she jumped. The article states that she left her parent's home about 3 a.m. but no source for this information is given. Three a.m., twelve hours after the death of Christ, is the designated time when evil is most powerful. Farnum descendants admit that Frances attended religious revival meetings in 1857. Seventh Day Adventists were actively and aggressively recruiting converts in Allegany County that year and Frances may have been strongly influenced by their religious beliefs. Was Frances Farnum upset by learning her father had withheld Gordon's correspondence? Was Frances Farnum troubled by Edwin Hall's poems of love and interest in marrying her while she still cared for Hanford? Did the religious revivals force Frances Farnum to believe that her *Philopena* flirtations with Mr. Hall violated Christian principles? Did Gordon's cold rejection of Frances because his letters were intercepted by her father lead to her suicide? There are no answers to these questions.

Hanford Lennox Gordon, whether or not he was in love with Frances Farnum, married the daughter of another lumber merchant, Sylvia Smith from Ceres, Pennsylvania a mere two months after the death of Frances Farnum. Nothing in the archive of the Gordon family references Frances Farnum. Hanford Lennox Gordon was married three times. His first wife, Sylvia Smith, died in 1877 in St. Cloud, Minnesota leaving behind a daughter. Gordon's second and third marriages ended in divorce. He fathered three additional children with his second wife. Hanford Gordon's will expressly forbids the burial of his second and third wives in the family plot in Los Angeles and banned the future burial of his son-in-law in the family lot, married to the daughter from Gordon's first marriage who predeceased her father. Gordon erected a major memorial marker in the cemetery in Ceres where his first wife grew up. The phrases on all four sides extol the virtues of first wife. Is this monument an attempt by Gordon to atone for not being a good husband?

Hanford Lennox Gordon suffered from tuberculosis his entire life. From 1875 to 1876 this illness confined Gordon to bed. During his confinement, he wrote his most well-known poem *Pauline*. His first wife died the next year and he dedicated this work to her. Gordon returned to Wellsville several times and at some point, a connection was made between *Pauline* and Frances Farnum. *Pauline* runs 120 pages. It explores Gordon's fights with the Sioux in Minnesota and his enlistment and years fighting for the Union in the Civil War. A portion of *Pauline* presents the tragic love story of Paul and Pauline caused by Pauline's father who forged letters from Paul (Gordon) rejecting Pauline (Frances?).

Memorial Stone for Gordon's first wife, Sylvia, at Ceres, NY cemetery

In turn, when Pauline learns of her father's perfidy, she contacts Paul who rejects her and Pauline commits suicide by drowning. This author believes that Gordon's dedication of *Pauline* to his wife is a strange commemoration given Sylvia Gordon did not die by drowning, but a possible first love in Gordon's life did. Did Gordon's fears of impending death resurrect unacknowledged memories about Frances Farnum's suicide?

Pauline gives credence to some of what is known about Frances Farnum, her possible friendship with Gordon, and the circumstances contributing to her death. Edward Farnum did not forge letters, but he did keep Gordon's correspondence from his daughter. Edward Farnum may have felt that Gordon's personality was not a good match for his daughter. Pauline was an only child while Frances was not. Paul meets his older successful rival for Pauline and learns that she is to marry him. In rejecting Pauline, Paul feels no guilt even though his actions may have contributed to Pauline's death. While Pauline committed suicide the morning of her wedding day, Farnum descendants note that Frances Farnum and Edwin Hall were not engaged and there was no wedding date. If Hanford Lennox Gordon did love Frances Farnum why did he so quickly marry a mere two months after Frances' suicide? Hanford and Sylvia Gordon left Allegany County for Minnesota soon after their marriage. Distance and a sudden marriage could have enabled Gordon to remove Frances from his memory. And, yet, he writes his most famous work about a young girl who commits suicide after being rejected by her preferred suitor.

Pauline by Hanford Lennox Gordon, published 1878

Autograph of Gordon inside 1878 copy of Pauline

Edwin Bradford Hall, daughter Fannie Hall Carpenter, and granddaughter, Florence Carpenter (Woelfel), 1900

Edwin Bradford Hall married Antoinette Farnum three years after the death of Frances Farnum. For a time, they resided in the Farnum family home. Construction on the *Pink House* did not begin until 1866. Hall descendants have been saddled with stories about the ghost of Frances Farnum haunting the *Pink House.* No reputable parapsychologist accepts that a ghost, if there are such things, haunts buildings that never existed in that person's lifetime. If Frances Farnum was to haunt a house it would have been her father's residence from which she left taking her own life. The Farnum house still exists and is divided into four apartments. Not one ghost story has ever emerged from this home. No one has ever seen the ghost of Frances Farnum in the *Pink House* either. The rumor that Edwin Hall rejected Frances for her more attractive younger sister Antoinette is just wrong! Antoinette was the oldest sister. There is no evidence that Edwin and Antoinette considered dating until long after Frances died. Given the content of Edwin Hall's Valentine poems to Frances Farnum, her suicide was a great blow both to him and her family, which took time to heal. The best testimony to the feelings, which Edwin Hall and Antoinette Farnum Hall held for Frances, is revealed in the name given to their only child, a daughter. They named their daughter Fannie, a variation of Frances!

CHAPTER FOUR

The Pink House | Exteriors and Ancillary Buildings

Edwin Bradford Hall and Antoinette Farnum married in Wellsville on June 5, 1860. Their honeymoon took them to Europe and the area around Lake Como in Italy. The traditional story about the origins of the Pink House claim that Mr. and Mrs. Hall based the design of the Pink House on one or more structures they saw around the Lake. This may be true but a book illustration on Bridgeport, Connecticut history reveals a house identical in appearance to Wellsville's Pink House, but built before Edwin Hall's.

The Pink House with its original chimneys with caretaker's wing on the right side of the residence

The Bridgeport house was the home of Eli J. Thompson, a close friend of P. T. Barnum. The Thompson residence was built in the early 1840s, painted white, and its image survives in only one sketch. Its design must have influenced Mr. Hall because it was located a mere 200 feet from his parent's house. Edwin Hall's Bridgeport neighborhood was one of small houses except for the Thompson residence and the house belonging to *Tom Thumb*. The Thompson residence was torn down in the late 1890s. No other records on the Thompson house survive. The Pink House survives from 1866 to the present day and was always painted in various shades of pink. Mr. Hall sold paint in his drug store, which was imported from Italy in the early days until he later mixed his own paint.

E. J. Thompson residence, Bridgeport, CT

After their honeymoon Edwin and Antoinette Hall resided with her family at the Farnum residence on West State Street. It was at the Farnum house that the Hall's only child, Fannie, was born on October 19, 1865. Realizing the need for a home of their own, Edwin Hall had engaged Rochester, New York architect Henry Searle to design a residence for his family. A May 18, 1865 receipt shows that Hall paid $125 for the architectural plans. The plans survive but suffered water damage in the late 20th century when water leaked into the Fossil House where the architectural drawings were stored. The site for his home was a four-acre plot on the corner

1866-69, Pink House under construction

of West State Street and West Main Street (now South Brooklyn Avenue). When construction started in 1866, there were no houses between the Farnum and the Hall residences. Construction of the original structure was completed in 1869 when the family moved in. The east side of the house was expanded from 1870s to 1880 to accommodate a music room on one side of the living room. This room had book shelves, a large desk, a very large stained-glass window and a grand piano. At the same time the family living room was expanded and a very large side porch added. On the second floor above two bedrooms with bathrooms were also added. In

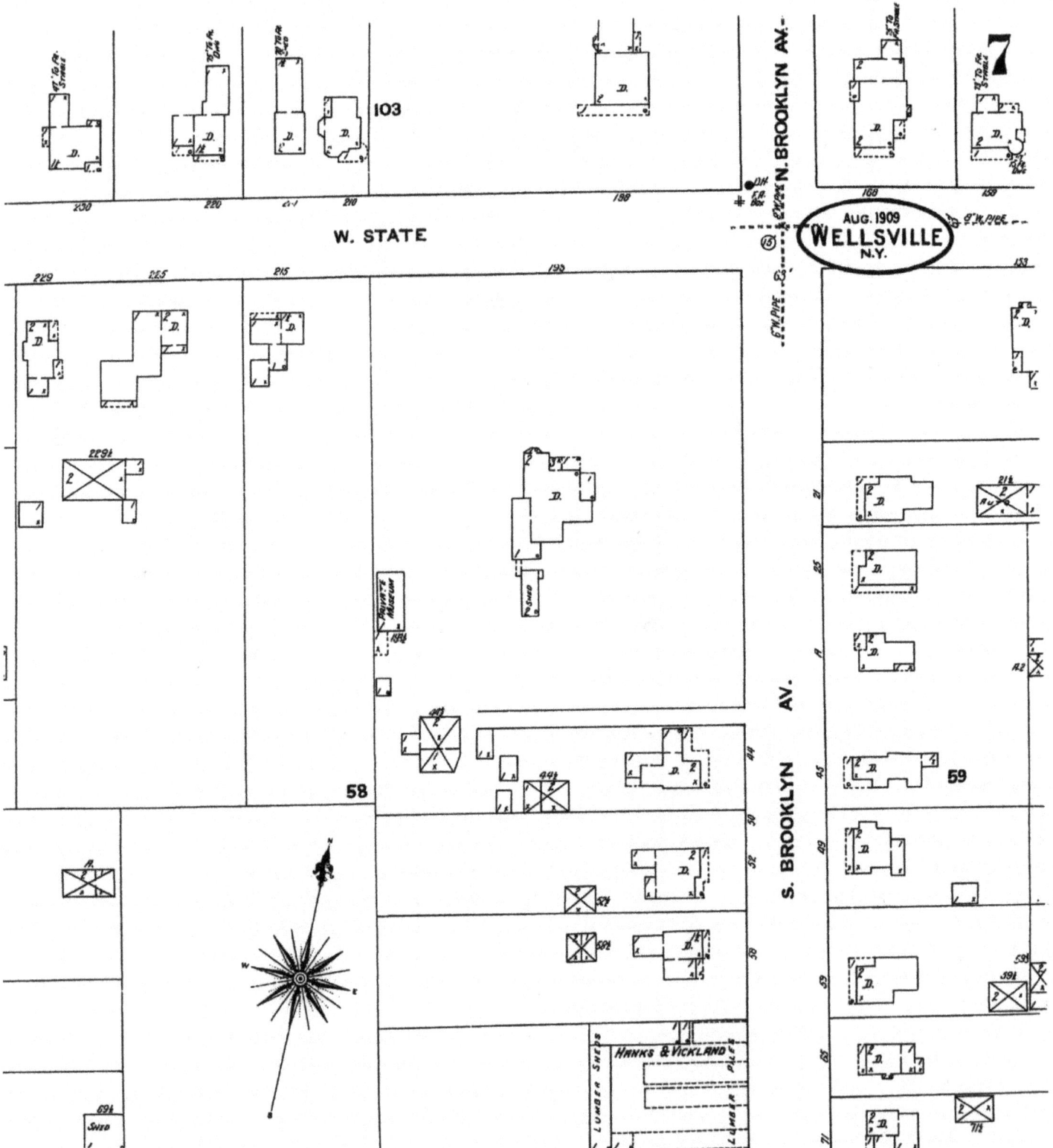

Sanborn Insurance Map, Wellsville 1907, E. B. Hall residence is shown in the center

the early 1900s the walkway between the kitchen and the ice house was taken down and replaced with a window because an electric refrigerator was installed and the original function of the ice house was no longer needed.

Final alterations to the Pink House came after John Milton Carpenter, Fannie's husband, died in 1926. Fannie had never been alone before and she needed more care. There had always been a housekeeper for the family.

1870s, Pink House with left to right, Mrs. Hall, Mr. Hall, and Fannie Hall seated on steps

1870s, Pink House from South Brooklyn Avenue before construction of Music Room showing the wooden fence

1870s, front view of the Pink House from the driveway before music room addition

Her only daughter, Florence Carpenter Woelfel (now married and residing with her husband in Baltimore, Maryland) came to help and she realized that Fannie needed a family living in the right-hand side of the residence who would always be there as additional caretakers and when the housekeeper had days off. This remains today as the *caretaker's apartment,* which has its own front porch and steps down to the driveway and to the back of the yard. The present caretaker is a school teacher in the local elementary school who is a great comfort to Julian and his wife because they, along with one son and his wife, and a niece, only visit in the summer and fall months.

1870s, sidewalk entrance pillars with garden urns to the left of the driveway

A closeup of the Hall family on the front porch during the 1870s

The Pink House is an Italianate villa style built around a central block and tower with wings and bays added. The exterior is flush board siding with sawdust for insulation. What makes the Pink House so unusual is the ornateness of the exterior around the windows, doors, and porches. The original roof was tin. The basement under the whole house has 3413 square feet with fourteen separate rooms with two furnaces and a separate door to the outside. The first and second floors each have 3244 square feet, and the third floor is the tower room, lined with chestnut wood, and ten feet square with very sturdy balconies with iron supports on all sides so it is safe to get out onto them to view the stars or other events like the annual balloon rally. Mr. Hall especially liked to study the skies. The Pink House is 1514 above sea level and is beautifully situated with an elongated design. Mr. Hall had the house built six feet higher than the ground to avoid the usual flooding from the nearby Genesee River. The flooding caused by Hurricane Agnes in 1972 forced the Army Corps of Engineers to move the Genesee River to prevent future high flood waters. The first floor consists of the double parlors, living and music rooms, dining room, kitchen, pantry, family room, and bedroom suite with bathroom. The second floor has six bedrooms, two large hallways, and two and one-half bathrooms. There are two staircases connecting the first and second floors. The third floor is the tower room. The caretaker's wing consists of six rooms with a large bathroom.

The Pink House in winter

The Pink House in winter at night

School children come from all around in October to *trick or treat* and graduating high school seniors, wedding parties, and other celebrants are welcome to have their pictures taken on the Pink House porch.

In the mid-1950s the side porch on the east side of the house was shortened to create a first-floor bedroom and bathroom near the kitchen because Fannie Carpenter was getting frail and had to have cataracts removed. Fannie Hall Carpenter died in the hospital at age 93 on October 13, 1958.

Pink House at Halloween with electrified statues

A gazebo and three ancillary buildings are also on the property. The gazebo or summer house on the east side is a round open structure with a green painted roof containing benches and tables. The design was copied from a building in Central Park in New York City.

Fannie Carpenter held tea parties and church gatherings at the gazebo lighted by Japanese lanterns. This structure has often been mistaken by locals for a well, which is actually on the other side of the house.

Gazebo often mistaken for a well on the side yard facing Brooklyn Avenue

The two-story ice house behind the main house is a wood frame structure with each floor 420 square feet. The first-floor stored ice cut from the Genesee River, which was hauled up through an opening in the second floor to be carried across a now dismantled walkway to the original kitchen. There is also a first-floor storeroom, a workshop, and a three-hole outhouse at the end.

The second floor of the ice house became a library and playroom when ice was no longer needed for refrigeration. The ice house was afterwards call the *playhouse* where Julian and his younger brother, Bruce, had toys there and played when his parents visited the Pink House. This was true for Julian's three sons as well.

Ice House and rear view of the Pink House with the first door (far left) opening to a staircase to the second floor, the second door opening into a storage room, the third and fourth doors opening into workshops, and the fifth door opening into a three-seat outhouse

Second floor of the ice house now used as a playhouse by two generations of Woelfel boys

Cross walk connecting the ice house with the main house, since dismantled

Ice House with three-seater enclosed outhouse on first floor

A one-story frame structure on the west side of the house was Edwin Hall's Fossil House. This building was probably constructed in the 1880s and does not appear on the Sanborn Insurance Maps for Wellsville until the beginning of the 20th century. The building consisted of 960 square feet divided into two rooms. One room served as an office/library and the other room housed over 5500 locally collected Paleozoic fossils.

Carriage House with Bradford Pear tree showing the wide entrance for carriage entry from Brooklyn Avenue perspective

The three-story carriage house has a first floor of 1401 square feet, a second floor of 768 square feet, and a third floor of 384 square feet. The two upper floors were used for storage; the wood used for the second and third floor walls and ceilings is beautiful chestnut. The first-floor housed two horses and a Brougham carriage. The carriage was clearly a society vehicle with brass and glass lamps. The driver's seat was padded and plush lined seats accommodated four passengers. The carriage dates to the 1880s and was donated to the Rushford, New York Historical Society by Norman and Florence Carpenter Woelfel because the museum had a better storage space.

Carriage House rear view with barn door to bring the horse and carriage in or out

Carriage House third-floor attic lined with chestnut wood and used for storage

Bradford Brougham now at the Rushford, New York Museum

Dr. Julian Woelfel and son Jay in the Bradford Brougham

Edwin Hall planted a variety of trees on the property including Norway spruce, blue spruce, arbor vitae, hemlock, pine, sassafras, oak, maple, hawthorn, chestnut, hickory, black walnut, butternut, wild cherry, white birch, elm, pear, plum, choke cherry, quince, and a variety of apple trees. One section of the property was reserved for berries where gooseberries, blackberries, and red and yellow raspberries flourished. Myrtle, Chautauqua Grass, and Golden Chain were planted along with an experimental Indian herb garden. At one time, there was a lawn tennis court but the space has been reincorporated into lawn. A Mountain Laurel bush planted at the time of Fannie Hall's marriage to John Milton Carpenter in 1894 continues to flourish on the front west side of the house by the driveway.

View of the circular driveway from the Tower Room

Dr. Julian Woelfel standing by one of two electrified Cornucopia at the driveway entrance to the Pink House and the Fiske Company metal label at the bottom

The main entrance to the Pink House is on West State Street although there is a back entrance leading to the carriage house on South Brooklyn Avenue. Italian female statues known as *Cornucopia* and purchased from the Fiske Company catalogue of New York City by Mr. Hall are atop columns on each side of the circular driveway entrance to greet visitors.

51

As a young boy, Wellsville resident, Dow Stannard, was playing hide and seek around the Pink House. He discovered that one of the statues had been taken down for repairs. He looked into the hollow base and decided he had found the perfect place to hide. Dow lowered himself from the top into the wooden base, dropping to the bottom. Then he discovered that he could not get himself out of the base and began hollering for help. Eventually, his cries were heard and an adult neighbor, Tom Stiles, came to his rescue pulling Dow Stannard up by his wrist. The statues were electrified with ball shaped white lights by Julian and Marcile Woelfel after Florence Woelfel's death in 1984. At one-time pairs of similar columns were placed to the left and right of the driveway entrance marking walking path entrances to the Pink House. Large planters were atop those columns. Age and replacement costs forced the removal of these columns but the planters have been recycled in the gardens. The driveway went around a large fountain with white metal planters. The fountain was dismantled after the death of Beatrice Carpenter in 1907 and replaced with a memorial garden. A beautiful wooden fence went along the entire property with gates for the entrances. However, the fence had to be removed in the 1950s because it was rotting and too expensive to replace. Black metal fencing behind shrubbery currently marks the property boundaries. A number of lawn ornamentals, including a deer, succumbed to old age and were not replaced. Two large lions guard either side of the steps leading to the front door. They were originally painted yellow but the color seemed to frighten horses, so they were later painted gray. The initial H in old-English style is carved above the front porch arch leading to the front door.

The Pink House casting a shadow across the front yard

Hall initial H above front porch arch leading to the entry door, in Old English style

One of a pair of grey metal lions guarding the Pink House on each side of the front steps

Pink House tower with walkout balconies

There is no answer to the question why Mr. Hall selected the color pink for his house. It was rumored that the pink paint was a special formula imported from Italy. The paint formula was created by Mr. Hall himself and he mixed it at the drug store he owned. The variations of pink have changed over time and during the 1960s the exterior was actually painted mauve before reverting back to pink. Edwin Bradford Hall was a creative businessman. Whatever rumors and stories were circulating about the Pink House, they went unanswered. Perhaps, that was Mr. Hall's intention because it kept his name and his business in the public's mind.

Pink House paint formula in Mr. Hall's handwriting

CHARTER FIVE

Pink House Details | The Interior Spaces

Edwin Bradford Hall and his wife, Antoinette, furnished their residence with Victorian era furniture. Many items were ordered from catalogues. Some items were specially made by master craftsmen for the house. It is the family's understanding that except for the furniture in the double parlors or blue room, some of the furnishings in the music room and the dining room, the furniture on the first floor was changed and the bedroom furniture moved from room to room or changed to more contemporary looks by each generation's preferences.

1885, Double Parlor of the Pink House, Mrs. Hall and Fanny Hall

Four photographs from the Hall era survive. Two of the photographs show opposite ends of the double parlors with Mrs. Hall and her daughter, Fannie, seated in each. The third picture is the music room with a seated Fannie. The fourth photograph is of the double parlors for the wedding of Fannie Hall to John Milton Carpenter. From the Carpenter era, there are photographs of the dining room decorated for Christmas and birthdays.

1885, Double Parlor looking toward the bay window, Mrs. Hall and Fanny Hall

1885, Music Room with a young Fannie Hall

1894, Double Parlors decorated for the wedding of Fannie Hall to John Milton Carpenter

With Dr. Julian Woelfel's retirement in 1995, he and Marcile were able to spend longer periods in Wellsville. It is the efforts of both of these exceptional people that began the process of restoration in keeping with the era when Edwin and Antoinette Hall were in residence. Original wall paper was reproduced, paint colors researched, gas chandeliers electrified, and Victorian era furniture restored and reupholstered. Marcile Woelfel made the final decisions on where the furniture was placed in each one of the rooms and her choices bring a beautiful interpretation of the Victorian period back to the Hall residence. The color photographs for this chapter were taken by Dr. Julian Woelfel when the Pink House welcomed guests for a fundraising event for Wellsville's Jones Memorial Hospital in August 2014.

Entry into the Pink House is through *coffin* doors. Funerals were held in the home and the double entry doors were wide enough for pall bearers to carry a coffin in and out of the house. On the staircase leading to the second floor is a gas light brass cavalier with a removable sword. Walnut wood carvings over the parlor door include a Griffon Bird Head, the Farnum family crest. Black walnut and seasoned chestnut woods are used in the staircase thresholds and railings.

Foyer with formal second floor staircase, gas-lit cavalier lamp, and the statue of Hebe on the landing

Over the opposite door is a seashell carving in the middle and on the stair step wall small grape clusters. German immigrants traveled through Allegany County and Wellsville in the last part of the 19th century bringing their wood carving skills. German master carvers Frederick Gaethe and his son, Otto, did the Pink House carvings. They also carved the altars for the old Lutheran Church, which were not saved when that structure was torn down. Along the downstairs hall walls are photographs of the family. A white zinc metal swan that once swam in the fountain in front of the house now graces a hall table, its paint removed. An oval wooden picture frame made of black walnut is an exceptional example of Yankee *whittling*. It was made by Mr. L. D. Hurd of Wellsville and is composed of 225 pieces with each piece representing the badge of either the 2nd, 6th, 9th, or 20th Army Corp. Four were carved by Mr. Hurd while a prisoner in Andersonville prison using Irish brigade symbols with shamrocks and shields and held together with interlocking pieces of wood. This one was gifted to Mr. Hall by Mr. Hurd. Today the frame displays photographs of John Milton Carpenter's family. The statue at the top of the stairs is the goddess *Hebe*, cupbearer to the Gods. This is a replica of the original in the Metropolitan Museum of Art.

Statue of Hebe on second floor landing. The original is in the New York Metropolitan Museum of Art. Visitors placed coins in the flat cup for good luck

Exceptional example of Whittling made into a frame containing photographs of J. Milton Carpenter's relatives on the "Ancestor Wall"

Back of the frame showing the hand carved interlocking components

Front Blue Parlor showing original chandelier with smoked glass bells for gas lighting

The double parlors on the right side of the entry hall are also called the Blue Room because of its many blue accents and the blue satin upholstery of the furniture. These rooms are the most elegant in the house and were used for weddings, funerals, and special family gatherings. It is divided into two rooms by a highly carved, elegant divider topped with a gold cornice matching the gold cornices above the windows in both rooms. The room is characterized by high ceilings and floor to ceiling windows with wooden shutters. Tall mirrors grace the room with their gold leaf cornices. One floor to ceiling mirror was hand painted with roses by Louise Farnum Brown, Mrs. Hall's younger sister. It can

be seen on the left side of the back-parlor wall. Most of the German porcelain pieces in these rooms were wedding gifts to the Halls. All the chandeliers are original to the house and were originally lit with oil; then gas after its discovery in nearby Potter County, Pennsylvania. The fireplaces used wood or coal until natural gas was available. After the discovery of oil and gas in Allegany County, Wellsville and the Pink House were among the first to have gas lighting and gas heat. The glass globes on the chandeliers are decorated with herons and flowers. The two white wooden columns are carved with small birds, ivy, flowers, and herons at the base.

Blue Room entrance showing marble fireplace and portraits of Fannie Hall Carpenter (left) and Frances Farnum (right) of the fireplace

Because Edwin Hall was interested in nature, plants, herbs, fossils, the sea, and the stars, many carvings throughout the house reflect his interests. The white Italian marble fireplace mantle holds two tall Italian imported alabaster urns and two painted bisque figures of a boy and a girl carrying their school books. Below the mantle is a seashell. The portrait to the left of the fireplace is Fannie Hall at the age of four painted by an itinerate painter from Pennsylvania. To the right of the fireplace is a portrait of Mrs. Hall's sister, Frances Farnum who died in 1857 at the age of 21 years. The landscape paintings in the double parlors are unsigned but were done by nieces of John Milton Carpenter, either Margaret Brown (1880-1950), Lillian Brown (1885-1954), or Ruth Brown (1887-1963). None of the sisters married. Their work shows a strong influence of *Luminist* painters Thomas Cole and Frederick Church. Three weddings have been held in the double parlors. Fannie Hall married John Milton Carpenter there in 1894 as did their daughter Florence to Norman Woelfel in 1924 and in 1972 the eldest son of Julian and Marcile Woelfel.

Part of the ornately carved room divider of flowers and birds with carved center decoration. The portrait to the left of the fire place is four-year old Fannie Hall (Carpenter)

White marble fireplace with alabaster urns acquired by Mr. and Mrs. Hall in the Blue Room

Alabaster urns purchased in Italy during the Hall honeymoon

Double Parlors bay window at the front of the residence

Ornate carved wood work dividing the Blue Room double parlors

In the dining room, a French tapestry named *Woodlands* hanging above the buffet was installed in 1926 covering the wooden cabinets and the service opening to the original kitchen. The door to the right of the tapestry was the entry point to the original kitchen. The dining table is set with pink Minton bone china and iridescent glassware. The hand-painted plates on the dining room walls were done by Fannie Hall Carpenter. A recessed cupboard holds glassware, china, and silver. There is a window in the dining room and this room opens on the left into a television room. The door to the left of the cupboard leads to the current kitchen, which replaced the original kitchen incorporated into the caretaker's wing. The caretaker's wing includes a new kitchen, living room, three large bedrooms, and a big bathroom.

Dining Room with Woodlands tapestry covering the original cupboards and pass through to the original kitchen

Across the hall from the long Blue Parlor Room is the family music room with the big stained-glass window adjoining the family room. In the Pink House the music room is dominated by a round stained-glass window and a larger painted window glass below, which might be polychromed, of tropical scenes. There is no explanation for why the Everglades motif was used for these windows. The room originally had a grand piano. The current piano came from the family home of John Milton Carpenter and holds a 1905 Edison phonograph with cylinders, a mandolin, and a violin. Fannie Hall Carpenter and her daughter, Florence, played and sang together at this instrument. The paintings are done by one of the Brown sisters. The music room area has the roll top desk used by Edwin Hall. A doll in a white dress is on display along with photographs of Fannie Hall and Florence Carpenter. On a small stand, next to the fireplace is a lamp with the figure of Swedish singer, Jenny Lind on the base. The fireplace floor tiles were made in Bennington, Vermont and the spittoons represent a bygone era of men gathering in a separate room from the ladies in the double parlors after dinner.

Library adjoining the music room with its stained-glass window

Music Room with the piano coming from home of John Milton Carpenter's family

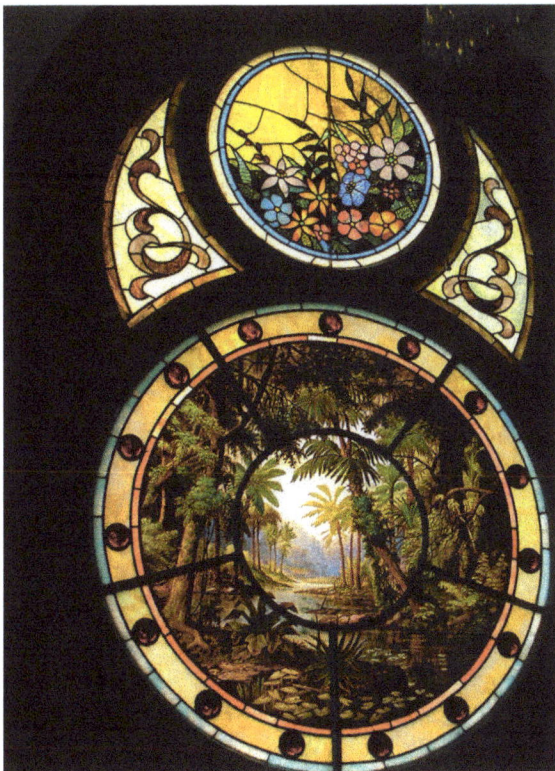

Painted, maybe, polychrome window with a stained-glass window above it in the Music Room

Edwin Hall's library with books on shelves and in the desk in the Music Room

Living room and a portion of Mr. Hall's library to the right with ornamental swam, which once floated in the fountain that once graced the front yard

Living room where the family gathered for more informal occasions

French style clock of Diana, Goddess of the Hunt with her arrows and dog atop living room marble fireplace

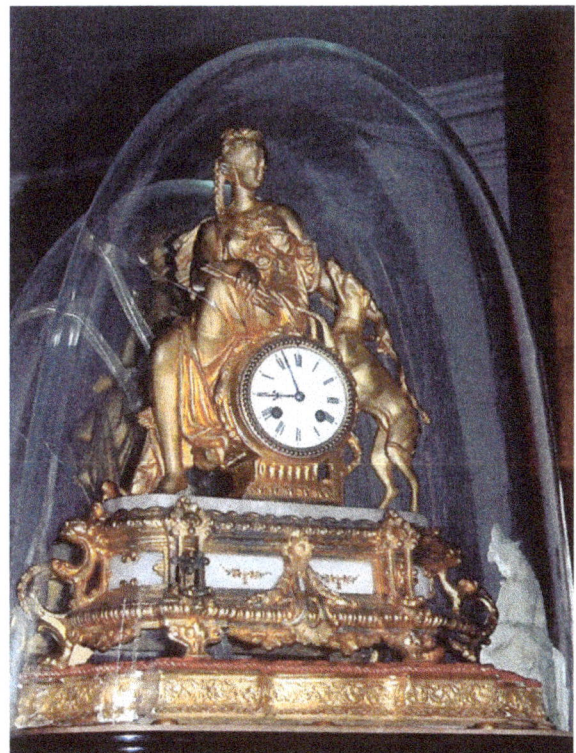

The front section of the second floor accommodates two bedrooms and is thirteen inches higher than the rest of the second-floor rooms in the back hall. Two floor-to-ceiling doors with colored glass panels on the upper portion and clear class on the lower part open to allow fresh air to circulate. When these doors are opened along with the ceiling trap door in the tower, a 19th century version of air-conditioning is in operation. The two large doors with stained-glass panels access the two small porches with white railings matching those on the third-floor tower room above. Before electricity, a gas light in both this area and in the third-floor tower room above were left on all the time. The flickering light at night gave rise to false rumors that the house was haunted. A corner *what-not* shelf in the hall is decorated with real acorns, leather leaf trim, and glass grapes. On the top shelf are white bisque children wearing large hats. A chandelier with electric globes facing downward is from the early 1900s and was the first to use electricity. This fixture could also burn gas in the top hall in case electricity was unreliable. Near the stairs leading to the tower is an antique bird cage on top of a chestnut wood chest where the chamber pot was stored before plumbing. The Empire drop-leaf table has an original Battenberg embroidery cover and holds an old-fashioned book of flowers.

Second floor hallway sitting room with staircase to the third-floor tower room. The stained-glass and clear glass doors open to permit air circulation from the tower room to the second floor

The pink master bedroom suite above the double parlors was used by Mr. and Mrs. Hall. This room enjoys thirteen-foot-high ceilings and has a wall paper border of maroon and green colors repeated in the oriental carpets and baseboards. Gold leaf moldings are found in both the bedroom and the sitting room in this suite. Wooden shutters are used for privacy and to keep out both the cold and the sun. The middle window pane has bubbling, typical of hand-made glass. A large black walnut bed and dresser are against one wall and additional dressers are on either side of the marble fireplace. The sitting room has a red velvet settee and chairs. The settee was once downstairs and upon it was laid the body of baby Beatrice Carpenter. A small writing desk has a cross-stitched Pink House picture above it. A door leads to a small bathroom. Mr. Hall installed a sink in each bedroom for the room's occupant to use, a very modern feature in the house at the time.

Mr. and Mrs. Hall's Pink Bedroom with thirteen-foot ceilings

Upstairs Pink Bedroom suite of Mr. and Mrs. Hall on second-floor front landing

Pink Bedroom suite sitting room with the couch on the left on which Beatrice Carpenter was laid out. The Pink Bedroom is on the second-floor front landing

Fannie Hall's bedroom as a young girl across the second-floor hallway from Mr. and Mrs. Hall's bedroom

The room across from the master bedroom on the second-floor upper hall is the blue bedroom. A walnut bed is between closets hung with drapery rather than doors. Florence Carpenter Woelfel's sled with swans on top of runners is placed near the bed and photographs of her around 1900 are in evidence. A Lincoln rocker and an Empire dresser with mirror with two small oil lamps complete this room. It is believed that Fannie Hall Carpenter used this room as a young girl.

A door opens to the back-upstairs hallway where there are three bedrooms, two bathrooms, and a former sun room. The first door on the right opens to a full bathroom with a stained-glass window titled *The Long Journey Home*. The last door on the right of this back hall opens into what was the *Sun Room*. The two side windows could be opened with rope pulleys to the ceiling to allow sun bathing in private. Mr. Hall and Mr. Carpenter, both pharmacists, believed in the value of sunshine and vitamin C.

Hallway to more family bedrooms on the back second floor hallway with lower ceilings

The back second-floor hall contains the *Ancestor Wall* of family photographs for five generations of Hall-Carpenter-Woelfel members. A blue and white quilt named *Feather Star* hangs on one wall and a framed print of a Maxwell Parrish painting of ladies in 1920s attire on the opposite wall. An antique teacher's desk with a gold-framed mirror and two leather chairs are across from the bathroom on the right side of the hall.

Stained glass window named The Long Journey Home in the second-floor bathroom adjacent to Florence and Norman Woelfel's bedroom

The second right hand door opens into a bay window bedroom with window seats under stained-glass windows. This room is paneled to the tastes of Florence and Norman Woelfel who used this bedroom during their Pink House stays. A dresser has a carved lady's head above the mirror and two lion heads with green beaded eyes on the side of the mirror. Teardrop pulls are on the dresser drawers. A large rocker has gold-painted dragons. Views from the bay window show the Fossil House and Ice House.

Florence and Norman Woelfel's bedroom with a small writing desk with a drop-down lid to the left of the bay window and the door to their bathroom on the opposite wall

Bay window in Florence and Norman Woelfel's bedroom on the right side of the second-floor back hall with stained glass panels on the top of each bay window. The five window seats below with green velvet seats are for storage

The Yellow Bedroom suite of Mrs. Fannie Carpenter's showing the bedroom and sitting room with fainting couch

The first door on the left side of the lower second floor hall opens into the Yellow Bedroom and sitting room used by Fannie Hall Carpenter and decorated in the 1920s style. This motif is repeated on the white built-in drawers on the opposite wall. The black marble fireplace on the left in the adjoining sitting room is decorated with *tic-tack-toes*. Two framed Gasdorf prints of the Pink House in autumn and winter are on the wall. The blue velvet fainting couch dominates the sitting room. Fainting Couches were necessary for too tightly corseted women. A wicker tea cart is near the fainting couch. Two rockers offer inviting spaces to read books and magazines from the nearby shelves or to watch television. A balloon rally poster featuring the Pink House hangs near the fireplace.

Mrs. Fannie Carpenter's sitting room in the Yellow Bedroom with book cases. The windows look down on the gardens and gazebo on the Brooklyn Avenue side of the residence

The second door on the left opens into the housekeeper's bedroom with a suite of matching oak Victorian era furniture. The last room on the left is the housekeeper's bathroom, original to the house, with a full-length stained-glass window with orange lilies topped with a hand carved cornice that came from the Carpenter family home. A pull-down gas lite with etched blue glass globes, had to be lit with a match. The old wooden toilet with a wooden water tank above it were replaced. A claw-footed bath tub is painted gold but is *not* made of gold as rumors once circulated.

Housekeeper's bathroom with original blue-globe gas lit chandelier, gold painted tub and stained-glass window

Carved cornice over second floor stained-glass window in the housekeeper's bathroom window. The cornice was originally in the Carpenter residence on Main Street

The stained-glass window in the housekeeper's bathroom

The second-floor landing stairs lead to the third-floor Tower Room. The Tower Room is ten feet square with balconies and windows on each side. The balconies are supported and reinforced with metal so a person could come out the windows and stand on the balconies. Mr. Hall liked to observe and study the stars. Mrs. Marcile Woelfel would wave to balloonists as they passed by the Pink House during Wellsville's annual June balloon rally. The spire atop the Tower Room is wooden with gold trim and serves as a lightning rod connected to the ground on the west side of the house. The Tower Room contains a doll's house made from a drug store crate for Florence Carpenter Woelfel and other toys. This space was a favorite for the children of the house. The window views offer a variety of perspectives of Wellsville and at night star-gazing.

Second floor hallway with staircase to the third-floor tower room.

Tower Room with doll house made for Fannie Hall. Behind the doll house is the ascending staircase to the tower

Tower Room child's toy horse pulling a Borden milk wagon

Tower Room children's toys showing two of the four tower room windows which open to allow permit air circulation from the third to the second-floor rooms

Tower Room children's tea service on doll truck with doll clothes hangers

A 19th century view from the Tower Room showing the original wooden fence with driveway gates, statues, and fountain with ornamental swan at the front of the Pink House

CHAPTER SIX

Edwin B. Hall | The Druggist

Edwin Hall's arrival in Wellsville in 1852, came one year after the arrival of the Erie Railroad's first trains. Mr. Hall studied to be a druggist in his native Connecticut where he gained certification. He renewed his certification in 1865 in accordance with New York State requirements. In the first year of operation the drug store was co-owned by Mr. Hall with his uncle, Clark Bradford. Hall purchased his uncle's interest in 1853 and the store became exclusively an E. B. Hall enterprise. Hall's first drug store was located on Main Street across from the First Congregational Church.

Exterior view of Hall's Drug Store, 1885 at the time E. B. Hall gave the running of the store to his son-in-law Milton Carpenter; L to R: Ross McClure, Milton Carpenter

93

Interior view of Hall's Drug Store, 1909, L to R: Ross McClure, Keith E. Harris, partners and customers Leon Wyant and clerk A. Byron McClure

In 1857, Hall's Drug Store moved to the Union Block at 176 North Main Street across the street from the Brunswick Hotel. An 1867 fire destroyed the building, but Mr. Hall rebuilt his business as a brick structure and the store remained there until its closure in 1974.

Hall's Drug Store was more than a pharmacy. It sold a variety of items including paint, oils, glass, linseed oil, spirits of turpentine, chewing tobacco, and white and French zinc. Other products for sale included furniture varnish, kerosene, hair renewer, and liquor. Mr. Hall paid $75.00 in April 1898 to Allegany County for the right to sale liquor. More exotic products for sale included dynamite, Mrs. Winslow's soothing syrup, Kennedy's medical discovery, opium, and morphine. To attract ladies, the drug store offered toiletries, perfume, and fine soaps. An 1875 description recorded that Hall's Drug Store was one of the finest stores in Western New York. The window panes were ½ inch thick and completely clear. The glass was reputedly imported from France. Edwin Hall was known as one of the finest chemists in the area taking great pains to procure ingredients for his prescriptions. It is interesting to note how many prescriptions included some form of alcohol.

E. B. Hall drug store on Main Street at the turn of the century

Song book for sale at E. B. Hall's Drug Store

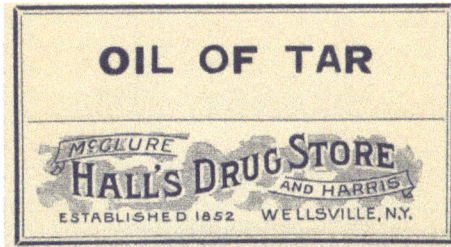

Hall's Drug Store advertising labels

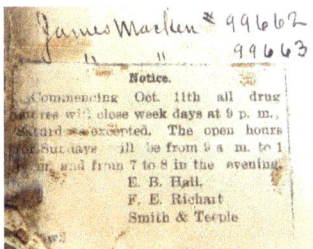

Hall's Drug Store hours of operation

Liquor Tax Certificate for E.B. Hall, 1898

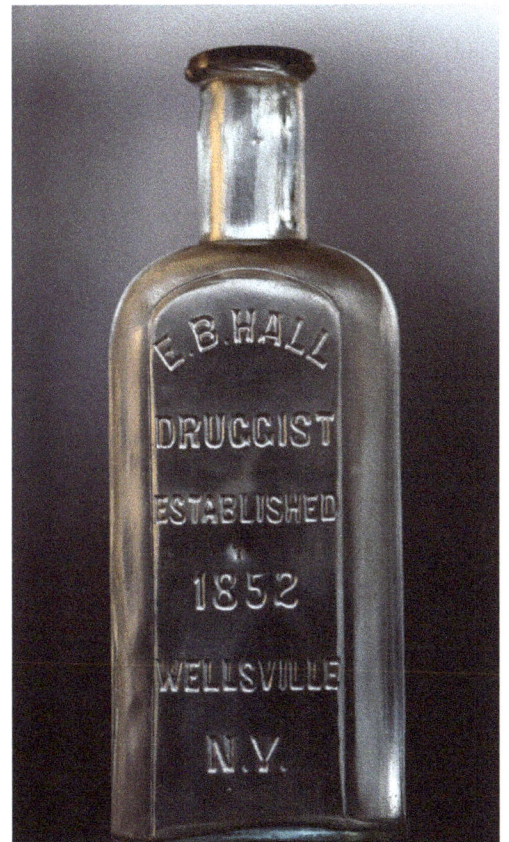

Hall's Drug Store medicine bottle, established 1852

95

Circus entrepreneur P.T. Barnum was like Edwin B. Hall, a native of Bridgeport, Connecticut. It is not known if the two men ever met, but Edwin Hall knew how to advertise to attract customers just as Barnum did. Edwin Hall was one of the first merchants to advertise in local newspapers. Copies of *The Democrat* record Hall Drug Store advertisements as early as 1869. The first soda fountain in Wellsville was in Hall's Drug Store serving flavor charged water drinks, but not ice cream. Customers came in to hear Mr. Hall's singing mouse—yes, a mouse that apparently did sing! With purchases, he gave away Victorian trading cards.

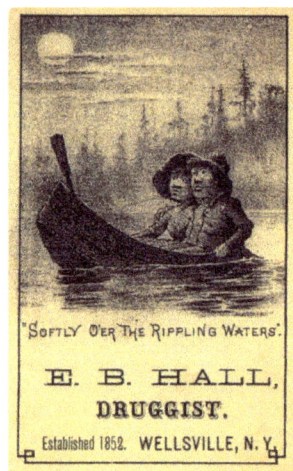

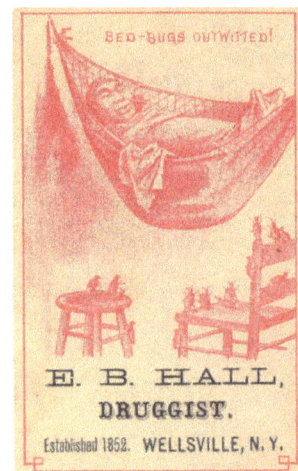

Victorian Trading Cards given with Hall's Drug Store purchases

When rumors swept Wellsville that Confederate forces, already in Gettysburg, might be headed further north, Hall installed a steel vault into the store's brick walls to secure valuables. The rebel army never came to Wellsville, but its residents appreciated Edwin Hall's foresight.

Hall's drug store had one of the first freight elevators in Wellsville. Supplies were loaded onto the elevator and raised to the second floor using a windlass operated by a 9-foot bull wheel. Customers came in just to watch the elevator in action. A pot-bellied stove invited customers to stay, sit, and smoke. The weather was a frequent topic of conversation as was politics. Boring weather conversation was a terrible distraction for Mr. Hall. Therefore, he rigged a wind vane on the top of the roof tied to a long rod which hung down inside a wall and reached to the first floor. In a store alcove a clock, four feet in diameter, was set up. A compass dial marked off 24 points. The pointer was connected to the dial and the wind vane shaft. The pointer swung in the direction of the incoming breeze. Edwin Hall's wind indicator predated the creation of the Weather Bureau in 1890. Much of the success of Hall's Drug Store is attributed to the savvy business skills Mr. Hall practiced to find new ways to bring the curious into his store to see what was new. Through innovation and advertising Edwin Hall never disappointed.

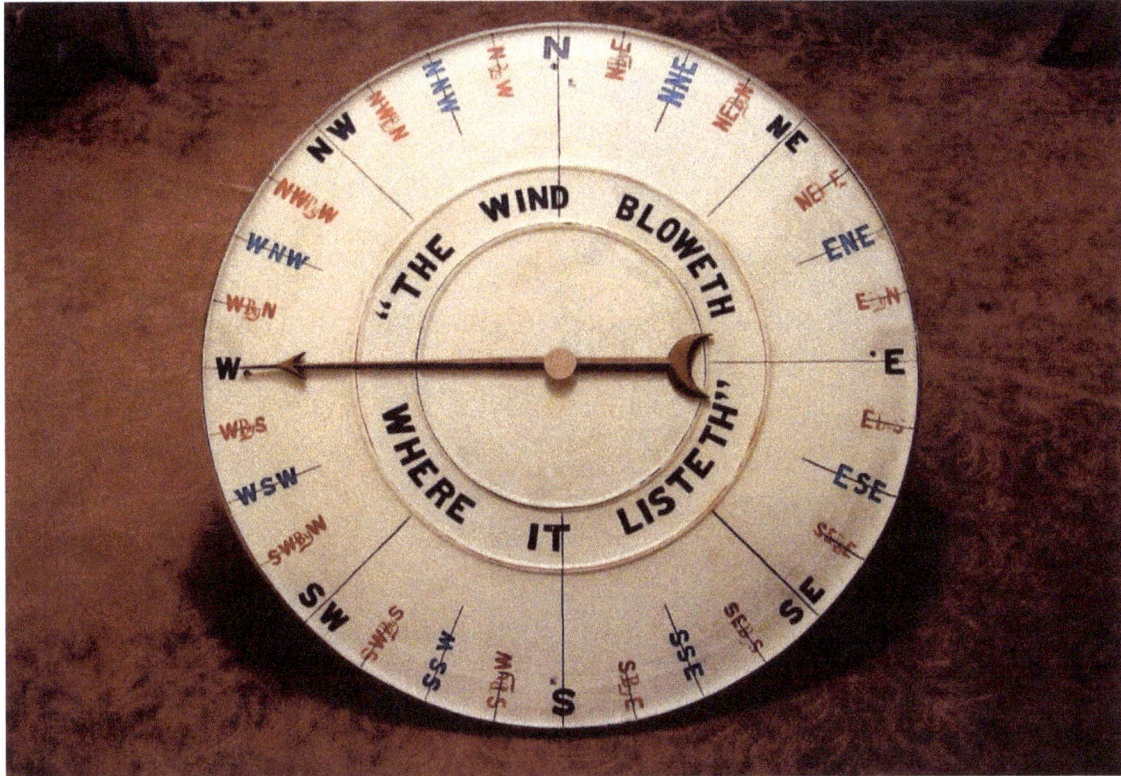

Weather indicator, Hall's Drug Store gifted by Julian and Marcile Woelfel to the Thelma Rogers Museum, Wellsville, New York

Prescriptions from E. B. Hall pharmacy book

John Milton Carpenter became an employee of Mr. Hall's about 1880 after obtaining his pharmacy license. Mr. Carpenter went on to marry the boss' daughter in 1894 and ran the business from 1894 until 1920 when he retired due to ill health. Employees Ross McClure and Keith Harris became the new co-owners running Hall's Drug Store until 1950 when Mr. McClure retired and sold his share to Keith Harris. Keith Harris owned and managed Hall's Drug Store until it closed in 1974.

It was a sad day for Wellsville when Hall's Drug Store went out of business. The two large glass containers, one per window, had been moved inside to the pharmacy counter and contained colored water. To a young boy, they were mesmerizing accessories to a drugstore because of their unusually large size and shape. They were sold along with all the store's fixtures. The pharmacy counter and a standalone unit with stained glass and drawers and shelves were purchased by a Westfield, New York antique shop and eventually found their way into the private home of Kathy and Bob Heimann. The Heimann's purchased three Hall Drug Store Pharmacy Books. Two were donated to Wellsville's Thelma Rogers Historical and Genealogical Society; the third was sold. The weather vane with its zinc dial was acquired by Dr. Julian and Marcile Woelfel who donated it to the Thelma Rogers Society. The building has served as a restaurant since the drug store's closure.

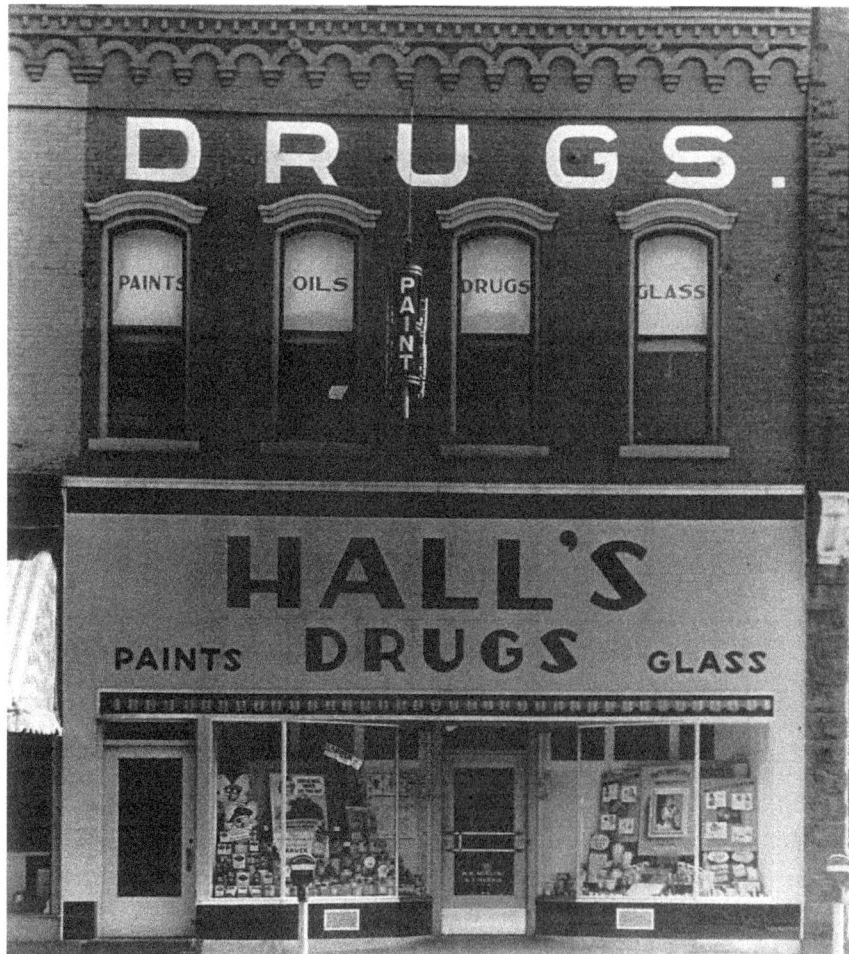

Hall's Drug Store, 1950s; now the Beef Haus restaurant

CHAPTER SEVEN

Edwin B. Hall | The Fossil Collecter

Edwin Bradford Hall's interests were limitless. When he moved to Wellsville in 1852, he actively collected fossil specimens around Allegany County. He was particularly interested in fossil sponges prevalent in the Devonian age period. Hall spend over fifty years collecting and the extensive number of specimens, over 5500, explains the construction of the fossil house to keep them. After the marriage of his daughter Fannie to John Milton Carpenter in 1894, Mr. Hall allowed his son-in-law to take over the operation of the drug store so he could spend more time with his collections. This allowed Mr. Hall the time to oversee the construction of the Fossil House to display and store his specimens.

Exterior, Fossil House

Office in Fossil House

Office showing entry to Fossil Room

One room in the Fossil House was Edwin Hall's office and a library exclusively devoted to publications about fossils, which numbered over 120 volumes. Among the books was a rare copy of *The Geology of New York, Survey of the Second District* by Ebenezer Emmons published in 1842 and an 1872 edition of Charles Lyell's *Principles of Geology*. In 1898, State Paleontologist James Hall (no relation) acknowledged in the Preface of *Memoir on the Paleozoic Reticulate Sponges* that he owed a great debt to Edwin B. Hall of Wellsville, New York whose cooperation was essential for the monograph's publication. In 1935 his daughter, Fannie, donated almost all of the fossil specimens to the Carnegie Museum in Pittsburgh where they remain on display. In 1996 Dr. Julian Woelfel gifted all of his great-grandfather's fossil library and the remaining fossils to the New York State Museum in Albany.

The second and larger room in the Fossil House was devoted to displaying and storing Hall's collection. An entrance on the left side of the Fossil House was large enough so wagons could back up to the building to be unloaded. The exterior back wall of the Fossil House was covered in metal to protect the structure from a possible fire from the candy factory on the neighboring property. The larger room originally had sky lights and an internal gutter system to absorb the moisture in the room emitted from the specimens. Mr. Hall was very systematic in organizing his collection with drawers specially designed to group specimens and with other specimens displayed on racks for further study. In an article *Edwin Bradford Hall* written by Reverend F. W. Beecher, the nephew of Harriet Beecher Stowe and minister at Wellsville's First Congregational Church, Hall was praised for his work as a scientist, observer, and investigator.

Fossil House, 2016 showing empty display cases and door on right side of the Fossil House

Fossil Room interior

Mr. Hall hired John S. Johnston to assist him in his fossil searches. Johnston was so successful that one formerly unknow specimen was named for him, *Thysanodictya Johnstonl.* There was no money to be made in collecting fossils. One collected because of the intense interest in the field. Edwin Hall did pay boys who brought in a new unseen specimen. There was no financial reward if the specimens had already been discovered. Edwin B. Hall's fossil sponge collection could be dated as far back as 300,000,000 years ago during the Paleozoic Era. They lived on the ocean floors when most of North America was covered with water. Shallow marine life thrived around Wellsville, making the area rich in fossil specimens. His sponge collecting went as far north as Bath and Avoca, east to Tioga County, and south into northern Pennsylvania.

Specimens common to the Wellsville area can still be found in waters near Japan and the Philippines. Mr. Hall was a self-trained botanist and geologist. He collected when there was an increasing interest in Devonian and Carboniferous formations in New York and Pennsylvania. Hall collected from specific areas in Allegany County that were untouched by human intrusion and before the county began to industrialize. Therefore, a tremendous debt is owed to Edwin Hall's foresight. The fossil specimens of prehistoric sponges proved that they were members of the animal, not plant, kingdom. Hall visited gorges and outgroups traveling to locations by train or stage coach, hiring a horse and buggy to get closer to the desired location and then undertaking a somewhat strenuous cross-country hike to reach the site. Hall checked off these locations on a map, which the family still has. Hall was so efficient that he took with him most of the existing specimens leaving future collectors empty-handed. A majority of his collection represented *Dictyospongidae* for upper Chemung rocks in New York State. Many from the Wellsville and Scio region are of the siliceous type; only one step above a one-cell animal. The sponges resemble the *Venus Flower Basket* with skeletons of thick glassy needles like basket work.

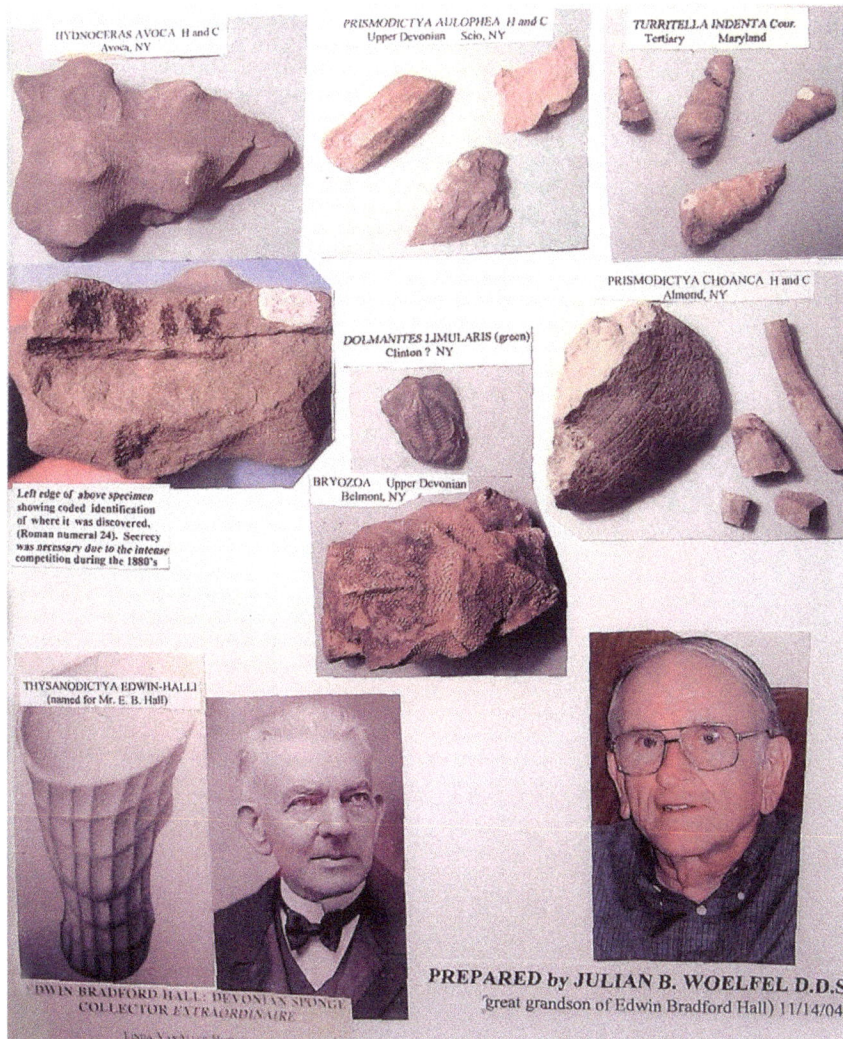

Fossil examples from exhibition organized by Dr. Julian Woelfel

Edwin Bradford Hall was elected to the American Association for the Advancement of Science in 1901 and in that same year Hall's collection was given first prize at the Pan-American exhibition in Buffalo, New York. Two specimens were named for Edwin B. Hall. The first was *Thysanodictya Edwin-Halli*. This was a small sponge found in the arenaceous beds of the Chemung group at Wellsville, New York. A hard to find species, Mr. Hall found it in considerable quantities locally. A second species named for Hall was *Thysandodictya Randalli, Hall*. This was from the Chemung group as well near Warren, Pennsylvania. A third fossil specimen was named for Fannie Hall Carpenter, his daughter, *Ceratodictya Carpenteriana*. This species was found on the Milo Cole farm near Ischua in Cattaraugus County. Edwin Hall donated eleven specimens of the *Dictyophyton Halli* from the Chemung group from Wellsville, New York to the British Museum of Natural History on August 8, 1890. In a further tribute to Edwin Hall a new genus and a new species were named for him: *Hallodictya* and *Thysanodictya Edwin-halli*, respectively. Edwin Bradford Hall made an incomparable contribution to the study of Geology.

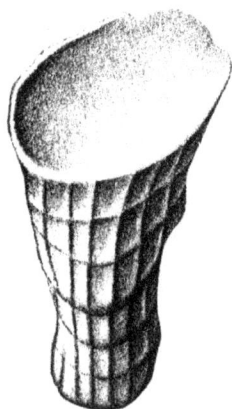

Thysanodictya Edwin-Halli, named for Edwin B. Hall, Edwin-Halli, all images

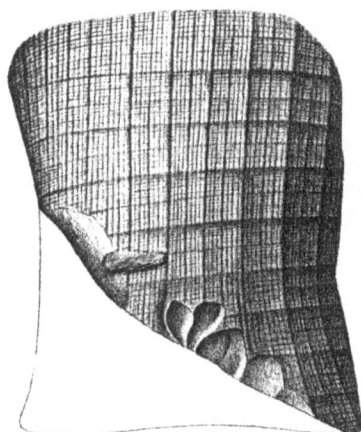

Thysanodictya Randalli-Hall, named for Edwin B. Hall

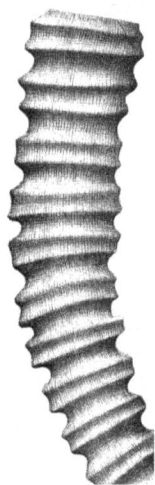

Ceratodictya Carpenteriana, named for Fannie Hall Carpenter

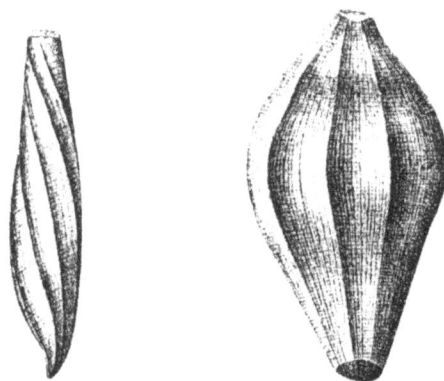

Ceratodictya Carpenteriana, two images, named for Fannie Hall Carpenter

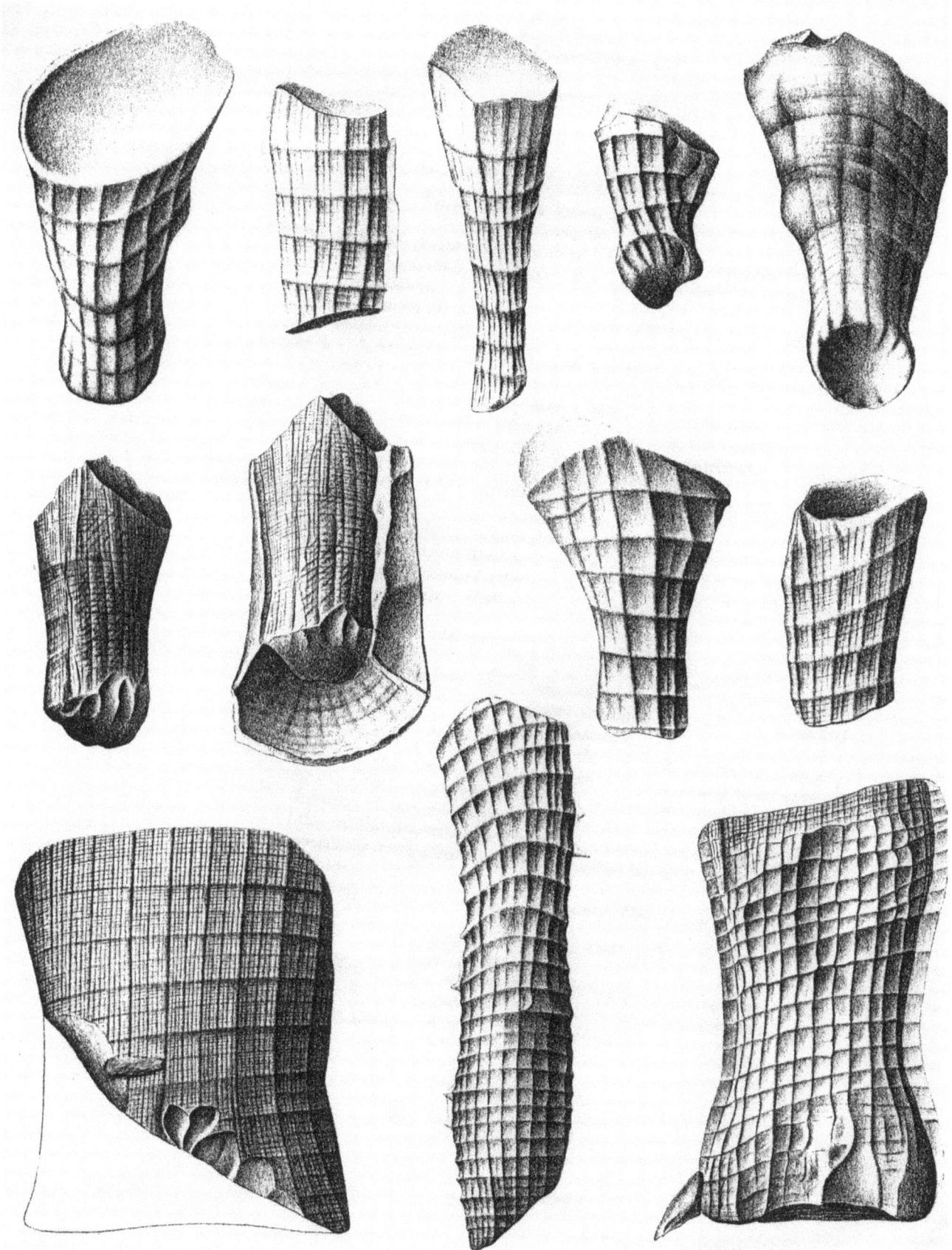

Thysanodictya Edwin-Halli, all images

CHAPTER EIGHT

Fannie and Milton Carpenter

Fannie Hall was born in Wellsville on October 19, 1865, the only child of Edwin Bradford and Antoinette Farnum Hall. Fannie resided at her maternal grandparent's house until the age of 5 when construction on the Pink House was completed. As a child there were no homes on the east side of West State Street between the Farnum and Hall residences.

Fannie married John Milton Carpenter on June 27, 1894 at the Pink House in the Blue Room or double parlors. John Milton Carpenter was born August 17, 1861 in Wellsville.

John Milton Carpenter as a young man

His father, John Carpenter, was a Wellsville merchant. His mother was Elizabeth Terry Carpenter. Mr. Carpenter was educated at Wellsville public schools. J. Milton Carpenter had two sisters, Lillian and Viola and two brothers, Whitfield and George. A third brother, John Carpenter, Jr., an infant, died in 1854. Viola married Watson Brown and it was her three daughters, Ruth, Lillian, and Margaret who did many of the paintings displayed in the downstairs formal rooms of the Pink House. Milton Carpenter's other siblings never married and resided at the family home on North Main Street until their deaths. J. Milton Carpenter received a degree from the National Institute of Pharmacy in Chicago in 1887. He found employment at Hall's Drug Store where he worked, married the boss' daughter, and ran the store for 40 years. Mr. Carpenter became interested in oil drilling, founded the Quintette Oil Company, and had successful wells in the townships of Alma, Willing, Independence, and Wellsville. The Independence well reputedly pumped 200 barrels a day. Milton Carpenter was an independent Republican, attended Wellsville's Congregational Church, and was a member of the Masons. He was a director of the First Trust Company Bank in Wellsville and was viewed as one of community's most prosperous and highly esteemed citizens. Carpenter belonged to the Country Club and each year he and his wife Fannie enjoyed traveling to Florida to engage in ocean fishing. Throughout his life, John Milton Carpenter was regarded as an upright and an honorable man and a staunch friend.

1894 Pink House wedding of Fannie Hall and Milton Carpenter, double parlors

Mountain Laurel bush planted in 1894 to commemorate Hall-Carpenter wedding

The wedding of Fannie Hall and Milton Carpenter united two of Wellsville's most admired and respected families. A mountain laurel bush (see photograph), planted on the front west side of the Pink House to commemorate their marriage, continues to thrive. The newlyweds honeymoon took them to New York City, Rome (Italy), Scotland, England, Paris, and Brussels. Upon their return the young couple took up residence in the Pink House. They had two daughters. Florence Lillian Carpenter was born April 24, 1898 and Beatrice Louise Carpenter on August 4, 1905.

109

Beatrice and Florence Carpenter seated on the Pink House steps

First Christmas for Beatrice Carpenter with her father, Milton Carpenter, and her sister, Florence

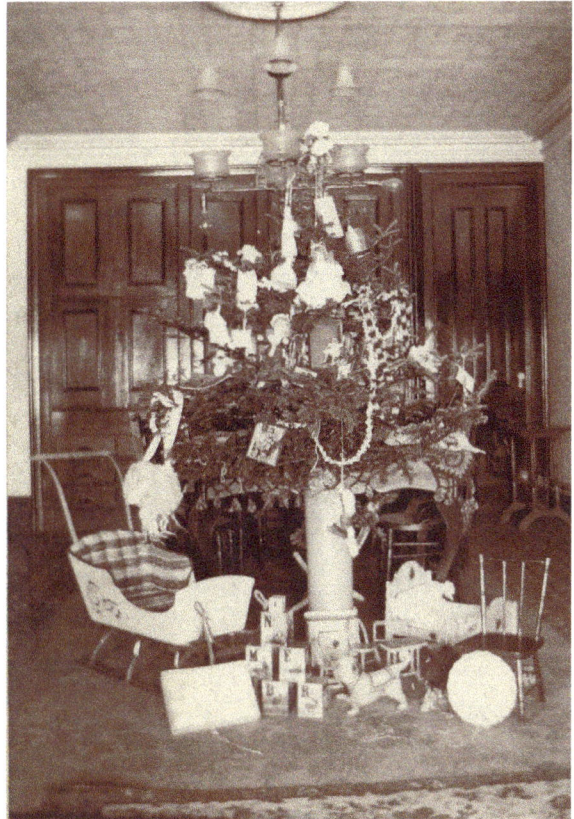

Dining room decorated for the holidays

Dining room decorated and set for Christmas

Beatrice Louise Carpenter died on September 28, 1907 at the age of 2 years. Beatrice drowned in the fountain that once graced the center of the circular driveway. Hall descendants believe that when Fannie Hall Carpenter opened the front door of the Pink House on September 28, to walk to the mailbox on the corner of West State Street and South Brooklyn Avenue, she believed that the heavy wooden doors had completely closed. Apparently, Beatrice discovered the door slightly ajar and was able to go out the front door and down the stairs toward the fountain. One Hall descendant believed that Beatrice might have been attracted to the life-sized white zinc swan ornament floating in the fountain, and attempting to reach out and touch it, tripped, hit her head on the fountain's concrete edge, and

fell face down into the water, and drowned. The fountain was not spraying that day, but there was water in the fountain. When Mrs. Carpenter walked back to the house, she discovered Beatrice face down in the water, pulled the child from the fountain, and screamed for help. Every effort was made to revive Beatrice including rolling the child over a nail keg. The doctors were unsuccessful in saving Beatrice. Mr. Hall was seated on the front porch but confined to a wheel chair and was unable to be of assistance in saving his granddaughter's life. Beatrice was an unusually pretty child with a sweet disposition whom everyone loved. The little girl was laid out in the Blue Room on a couch surrounded by banks of flowers.

Beatrice Carpenter in the middle with sister Florence on the right and a neighbor on the left at the fountain, 1906

Beatrice Carpenter, two years of age

The Hall-Carpenter family never fully recovered from the tragic death of baby Beatrice. Sometime after Beatrice's death, stories began to circulate attempting to connect the death of Mary Frances Farnum, the aunt of Mrs. Carpenter to Beatrice, both of whom drowned fifty years apart. The stories were both cruel and without foundation, but found their way into books about houses supposedly haunted. Edwin Bradford Hall died in 1908, his wife Antoinette in 1917, and J. Milton Carpenter died May 24, 1926 from complications from an appendectomy. With daughter Florence married and living away from home, Fannie Carpenter was alone except for a housekeeper. Soon after the death of Mr. Carpenter, the decision was made to convert several rooms on the west side of the house into a caretaker's apartment, which has remained so ever since.

J. Milton Carpenter seated on east side porch, now a bedroom

113

Fannie Hall Carpenter was actively involved in Wellsville's Monday Club and helped her aunt, Louise Farnum Brown, Monday Club President for 38 years (1896-1934), in getting the David A. Howe Library established. Fannie was a member of Allegany County's Garden Club where her interest in flora and fauna reflected a continuation of her father's interests in botany as evidenced in the landscaped yard and gardens at the Pink House. Mrs. Carpenter was a member of the Catherine Schuyler Chapter of the Daughters of the American Revolution. Fannie was a member of the first graduating class of Wellsville Public Schools to earn Regents diplomas. When in residence at the Pink House, Mrs. Carpenter had the exterior of the house beautifully decorated and outlined in lights during the Christmas season. An immense tree in the front lawn was lighted with hundreds of lights and the reflection of indirect lights gave the Pink House a fairy land quality. In earlier years Fannie Carpenter held small parties for groups at the gazebo decorated with Japanese lanterns. Mrs. Carpenter was described as a charming person with a lively sense of humor and a keen knowledge of the community and world affairs. She did regret never asking her father, Edwin Hall, more questions about the construction and decoration of the Pink House. To her, the Pink House was a place to live and was intrigued by people's fascination with her home. In 1935 Fannie Hall Carpenter donated 5500 fossil specimens from her father's collection in the Fossil House to the Carnegie Museum in Pittsburgh.

After the death of John Milton Carpenter, his widow, Fannie, decided to erect a mausoleum to contain the remains of her parents, husband, and infant daughter. The work was completed by 1929. When Fannie Hall Carpenter died in 1958, Beatrice's coffin was opened and Beatrice's remains were placed in her mother's coffin as Mrs. Carpenter requested.

Fanny Hall Carpenter in later years

John Milton Carpenter in later years

Florence Carpenter, Vassar graduate

Florence Carpenter, second from right, with friends

J. Milton Carpenter with fish he caught on annual trip to Florida, 1924/1925

CHAPTER NINE
The Woelfel Era

The death of Fannie Hall Carpenter on October 13, 1958 brought an end to the use of the Pink House as a full-time residence. The house, acreage, and ancillary buildings were left in Mrs. Carpenter's will to her grandsons, Julian and Bruce Woelfel, with daughter Florence having the right of lifetime use. For 90 years the Pink House has been occupied from one to four months a year by Woelfel descendants. The caretaker lives in the caretaker's apartment on the west side of the house, which was created in 1926 when Milton Carpenter, Fannie's husband, died.

Florence Carpenter Woelfel was an intellectually curious woman of whom her grandfather, Edwin Bradford Hall, would have been most proud. A graduate of Wellsville Central Schools, Florence Carpenter attended Vassar graduating with honors in 1920 and earned a Master's Degree from Columbia University in 1922.

Florence and Norman Woelfel in later years

Passing a rigorous examination, Florence entered the professional world as a clinical psychologist. Her accomplishments came as women earned the right to vote (1920) and established careers as independent women during the 1920s. Florence was a member of Phi Beta Kappa and the American Geographic Society.

Florence Carpenter met Norman Woelfel through mutual friends in Buffalo. Norman Woelfel, the son of Frank and Sophia Jungblut Woelfel, was born in New York City and raised in Buffalo, New York. Both sets of his grandparents came from Germany. Norman Woelfel had two younger brothers, Herbert and Elmer. The future Dr. Woelfel was a graduate of Buffalo Normal School and Columbia University.

He served in the 311th Infantry Division in France during World War I and began an illustrious career in Education teaching at Towson Normal School in Maryland as an instructor of psychology after returning home at the end of World War I. For 25 years Dr. Norman Woelfel taught education at Ohio State University in Columbus, Ohio. At Ohio State, Dr. Woelfel became a leader in promoting education via the radio in the 1940s and in the 1950s via television. By 1950, he was promoted to Chairman of the Teaching Aids Laboratory.

His Ph. D. dissertation was published by Columbia University Press in 1933 under the title *Critical Review of the Social Attitudes of Seventeen Leaders in American Education*. Professor Woelfel was a strong advocate that owners of television and radio stations and other forms of the media brought their bias to their media businesses influencing their readers and viewers.

Blue Room double parlors decorated for Carpenter-Woelfel wedding

Florence Carpenter Woelfel in wedding dress

Florence and Norman Woelfel on their wedding day October 25, 1924

Florence Carpenter and Norman Woelfel were married at the Pink House October 25, 1924. The Blue Room or double parlors once again became a wedding venue with the bay window transformed into a chancel. A stringed trio from Buffalo provided the music. The pastor of Wellsville's Congregational Church performed the ceremony. The reception was held at the house and numbered twenty-three guests.

Florence and Norman Woelfel's annual stays at the Pink House numbered one to three months. They occupied the upstairs bedroom with a bay window of stained glass looking out onto the gardens and the Fossil House. During their lifetime Florence and Norman Woelfel contributed funds for the expansion of the solaria at Jones Memorial Hospital. After Norman Woelfel's death in 1966, Florence deeded property on South Brooklyn Avenue to the Benevolent Association of Alfred. The land transfer was to accommodate expansion of the Wellsville Branch of Alfred Institute of Technology and to build campus housing for students on the property. Florence and Norman Woelfel gifted the Brougham carriage used by the Hall and Carpenter families to the Rushford Historical Society.

Florence Carpenter Woelfel and her bridesmaid, Hilda Reuning

The Pink House Blue Room decorated for the Carpenter-Woelfel wedding

Florence Carpenter Woelfel and Hilda Reuning in Blue Room

From Ohio, Florence and Norman Woelfel's love for and interest in Wellsville never wavered. Florence Carpenter Woelfel died in 1983 in Columbus, Ohio. She and her husband were interred in the Hall-Carpenter-Woelfel mausoleum in Wellsville's Woodlawn Cemetery.

Hall-Carpenter-Woelfel mausoleum Woodlawn Cemetery

121

Younger son, Bruce Everard Woelfel, was born on October 6, 1930. Bruce completed a degree in architecture at Ohio State University and moved to California to get a Master's Degree from Berkeley. Married twice, Bruce had two daughters, one son, and one adopted daughter from his first marriage. He and his children have all continued to reside in California. Bruce Woelfel sold his share of the Pink House to his brother Julian.

Julian Bradford Woelfel was born December 17, 1925 in Towson, Maryland. In 1937, the Woelfels moved to Columbus, Ohio where he attended the University School on the campus, graduating in 1943. He enrolled in the Ohio State University pre-dental Navy V12 Program graduating in 1948. World War II had ended by the time Julian graduated so he was no longer needed for military service. He joined the Ohio State Dental faculty as an intern in the denture department.

Norman and Florence Carpenter Woelfel with their sons Julian and Bruce

Wedding photograph of Julian and Marcile Cottrell Woelfel, Columbus, Ohio, 1948

Dr. Julian and Marcile Woelfel with their sons: Brad, Jack, and Jay

On May 1, 1948 Julian married Marcile Cottrell from Defiance County, Ohio. They met at a dance studio in Columbus where each was taking dancing instruction. Their marriage began an adventure of learning, teaching, and research travelling to professional meetings around the United States and to 18 foreign countries including the United Kingdom, Ireland, Turkey, Bulgaria, and Romania. For four months Dr. Woelfel taught at Nihon University in Tokyo in 1967. After Julian retired after 40 years at Ohio State University, he was a visiting Professor in Taiwan, Brazil, and London. He developed two denture patents which he later donated to Ohio State University. His textbook, *Dental Anatomy*, went into a 9th edition in 2017. For two years Dr. Woelfel was a research associate at the National Bureau of Standards in Washington, DC. Julian was a veteran of the Korean War and served as a Captain in the U.S. Army's 1st Armored Division at Ft. Hood, Texas where he ran the dental laboratory. Upon retirement in 1989 Julian and Marcile traveled to China, South America, Costa Rica, south Pacific islands, Europe, Africa, Madagascar, Easter Island and Papua, New Guinea. Together, they raised three sons, Bradford, Jack, and Jay.

Dr. Julian and Marcile Woelfel at Pink House front door

After Julian retired his and Marcile's annual stays at the Pink House increased to four months a year. Together, Julian and Marcile began the massive undertaking of restoring the Pink House. Leaking chimneys were removed and the tin roof was covered by a rubber membrane. All the layers of paint on the Pink House's exterior were removed and the original surface repaired and repainted. The ladies atop the driveway entrance columns were electrified. Inside the Pink House, wall papers were replaced, paint colors researched, and furniture restored and reupholstered. Gas lighting fixtures were electrified and layers of paint on glass windows removed. More contemporary furniture was removed from Pink House rooms and Victorian era furniture brought from the carriage house for use in their original settings. Much of the interior decoration and furniture placement was beautifully executed by Marcile. Decisions were made by Julian and Marcile to donate important historic items including books, manuscripts, and fossils to museums in New York State and Pennsylvania.

Dr. Julian Woelfel at Welcome to Wellsville sign with Pink House image

Not only was the Pink House restored, but Julian and Marcile brought the Pink House back into the life of the Wellsville community. For the last 30 years their Wellsville presence continued traditions that had ended with the death of Mrs. Carpenter. Ghost stories associated with the Pink House were debunked and set aside. On Halloween Julian enjoyed receiving neighborhood children into the Pink House. Entertaining brought Wellsville residents into the house removing a great deal of the mystery surrounding the structure and its history. In August 2014, the long years of restoration culminated in a fund raiser for the benefit of Wellsville's Jones Memorial Hospital on the grounds of the Pink House. Julian and Marcile made the Pink House once again a welcoming home for the 21st century as Edwin Bradford Hall did in constructing the house in the 19th century.

Dr. Julian and Marcile Woelfel in later years

125

JONES MEMORIAL HOSPITAL
"Pink Party"
Saturday, August 23rd, 2014
193 West State Street
Wellsville, New York

Pink House Invitation August 2014

Aug 23, 2014

2014, Pink House Party fundraiser for Wellsville's Jones Memorial Hospital

Dr. Julian Woelfel at Governor William Bradford monument in Plymouth, MA

Dr. Julian Woelfel's membership into the General Society of Mayflower Descendants as a documented descendant of Governor William Bradford

SOCIETY OF MAYFLOWER DESCENDANTS
IN THE STATE OF OHIO

DR. JULIAN BRADFORD WOELFEL
I have the honor to inform you that, at a
meeting of the Board of Assistants held on

DECEMBER 15, 2016
you were duly elected a member of the
Society of Mayflower Descendants

General # 90314   State # 3,500

Yours respectfully,
Jeddy Hunsell
Corresponding Secretary

Chapter Ten
Louise Farnum Brown

Louise Adelaide Farnum was born in Bath, New York on September 6, 1842, the sixth child of seven to Edward Judson Farnum and Lucy Goff Farnum. Little information survives about Louise's early life. On September 6, 1866, she married Alfred Stewart Brown, a successful Wellsville businessman. They resided at 129 North Main Street, between the Brown and Stout Insurance building and the original Congregational Church, a site later occupied by Loblaws grocery store and Rite Aid drugstore.

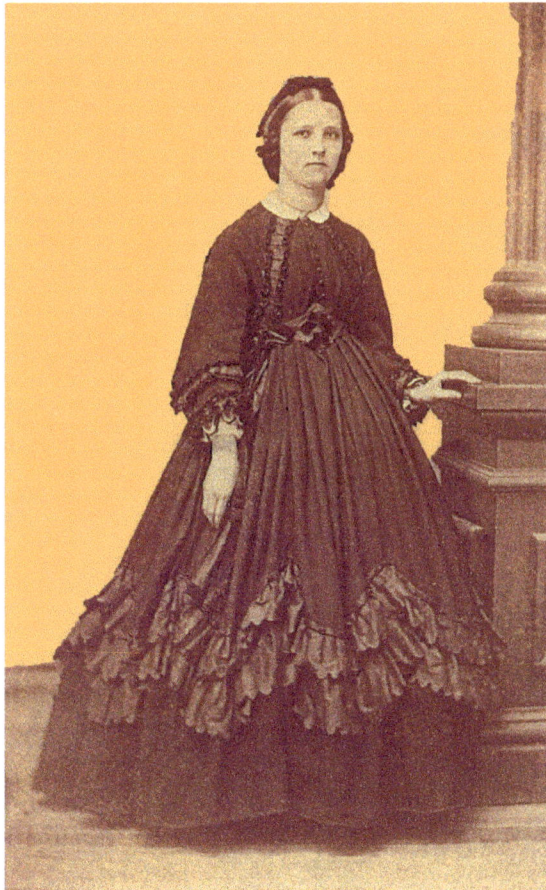

Louise Farnum, 1860s

Alfred Stewart Brown at the time of his marriage to Louise Farnum

Louise Farnum Brown at the time of her marriage to Alfred Brown

A son, Edward Carlton Brown, was born to Louise and Alfred on March 28, 1868. Louise was a talented artist, which can be witnessed by the painted long mirror in the *Pink House* double parlors of pink roses entwined and the hand painted blue satin decorations on the parlor chairs and couches.

Alfred Stewart Brown was involved in a number of Wellsville businesses including a dry goods store, lumber interests, and oil production. He was part owner of the *Wellsville Times*. Mr. Brown served three terms as President or Mayor of the Village of Wellsville, served five years as Postmaster for Wellsville originally appointed by President Arthur, and was a long serving member of the Wellsville school board. Alfred Brown constructed the Lincoln Block on Main Street, remodeled the post office and other older

buildings, which contributed to a more attractive downtown business district.

Louise Farnum Brown's fame originated with her push to establish a library for the village of Wellsville. On March 6, 1893, Louise Brown with twelve other women, submitted a constitution and by-laws for the creation of the *Monday Club*. The Club was organized to offer social and literary opportunities to their members and to create a public library. A previously existing public library in Wellsville had failed. The books were boxed and stored. A provisional charter for the Monday Club in 1894 allowed the organization to use a room in the local high school as a lending library. Community members provided the furniture and shelving.

Soon the library needed more space and was moved to two rooms in the City Hall when Alfred

Brown residence at 129 North Main Street to the left of the old Congregational Church with Alfred Brown (husband of Louise Farnum Brown) in the carriage, 1892

Brown was mayor. A permanent charter was granted to the Monday Club in 1897. Among the original membership of the Monday Club were Mrs. Mary Johnson Macken, Mrs. Mary Farnum Macken (a cousin), Mrs. Fannie Hall Carpenter (Louise's niece), Antoinette Farnum Hall (Louise's sister), and Sylvania Farnum (a sister).

In 1896 Louise Farnum Brown was elected President of the Monday Club, a position she held for 38 years until her death in 1934. Louise Brown exemplified many women of her era who were daughters and wives of wealthy businessmen who wanted to make a contribution to improve the lives of everyone in the community. Therefore, her push for a permanent library. The Monday Club membership donated their time, money, and spirit to achieve this goal. The society raised funds for the library by sponsoring concerts, lectures, card parties, teas, and selling old newspapers. The Club's commitment to a library generated many new members.

But, it was Louise's contacts with David A. Howe, her husband's nephew, that ultimately

Brown residence at 129 North Main Street, sold and razed in 1936

sealed the deal and brought Wellsville its first library building. Mr. Howe provided the $17,600 needed to construct the first David A. Howe Library and the Monday Club raised $3000 to provide furnishings and equipment. The library collection increased from the original 100 volumes the Monday Club had in storage to 4,340 books, maps, and periodicals when the library opened in 1910. The collection soon increased to 9,000 books. Louise was elected President of the Library's Board.

It was rumored that when David A. Howe asked his aunt how his *library child* was doing, Louise replied *she is growing but needs shoes and proper clothing*. Mr. Howe advised Louise to be patient. *Your child shall someday be sumptuously attired*. Louise displayed perseverance, determination, and generosity by indefatigable efforts to bring her dream of a center for learning, culture, and the arts to Wellsville. Nothing stopped Lou-

Louise Farnum Brown

Louise Farnum Brown, widow

ise including the early deaths of her husband, Alfred Brown on January 21, 1908, her beloved sister, Antoinette Farnum Brown on June 28, 1917, and her son, Edward Carlton Brown on March 8, 1932. Edward Carlton Brown's Tudor-style residence on North Main Street was once considered the most opulent home in Wellsville that all other residential property values were pegged to the Brown house.

Louise's patience paid off when David A. Howe left the bulk of his estate to fund a second library in Wellsville. At the age of 92, Louise fell at home, suffered a fractured hip, and died two weeks later on November 9, 1934. Louise Farnum Brown did not live to see the opening of the new and improved David A. Howe Public Library. A keen mind and an endless source of energy had departed Wellsville. Louise Brown's three grandchildren, J. Farnum Brown, Olin Brown, Dorothy Brown Comstock, and their descendants remained involved in the David A. Howe Public Library. Each generation provided Board members to continue the work Louise started. Her grandson, J. Farnum Brown, was President of the Library Board when the new structure opened in 1937. The Monday Club continues to thrive and contributes to the Wellsville community. Today, Louise Farnum Brown's descendant, Donald Comstock, serves on the Library Board.

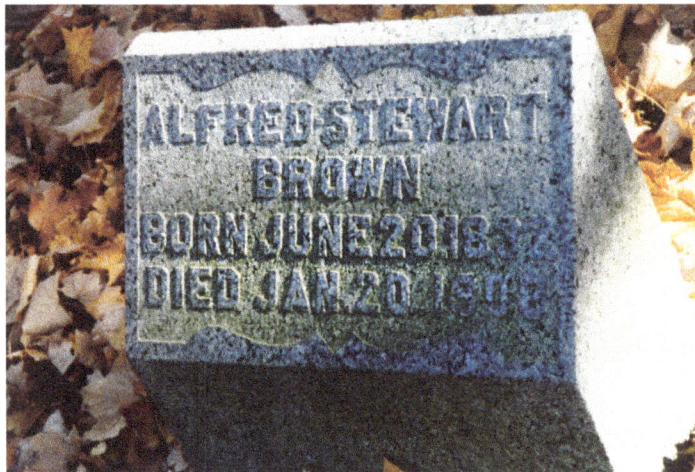

Grave Alfred Stewart Brown, Woodlawn Cemetery

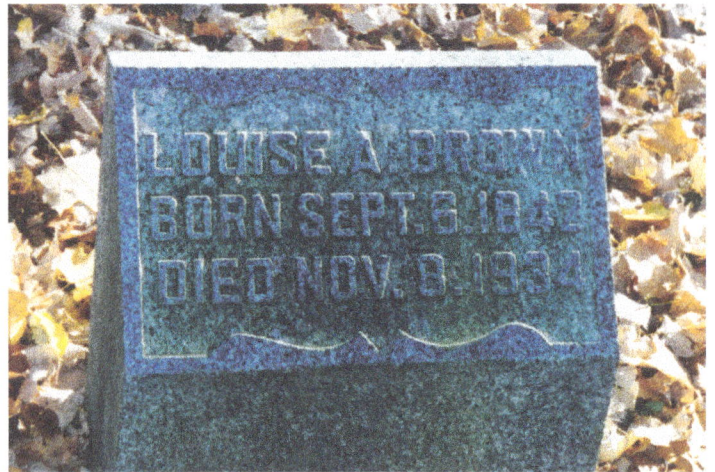

Grave Louise Farnum Brown, Woodlawn Cemetery

North Main Street residence of Edward Carlton Brown, Louise's only child. This residence remains on North Main Street with the exterior basically unchanged

CHAPTER ELEVEN
David A. Howe Public Library

David Abiram Howe was born in West Almond, New York on July 26, 1848. His father was a newspaper editor who moved to Wellsville in 1853 to run the *Wellsville Times*. Mr. Howe's uncle was Alfred Brown, husband of Louise Farnum Brown, who employed his nephew at his Wellsville dry goods store. After completing his educational studies at Dickinson Seminary in Williamsport, Pennsylvania, Mr. Howe married Wellsville resident Nan (Nancy) A. Reeser. They relocated to Pennsylvania where David A. Howe became a successful lumber merchant. His timber mills in the West Branch Valley became the largest operation in that area.

David A. Howe (1848-1925), nephew of Alfred and Louise Farnum Brown

1909 ground breaking for the first David A. Howe Public Library. Louise Farnum Brown seated center in second row

When timber production entered a decline, Mr. Howe shifted his financial interests to corporations, public utilities, and financial institutions. Returning to Williamsport, David A. Howe became part owner of the *Williamsport News*, was an active member of the Masonic Lodge, and was elected President of Williamsport's Brown Memorial Library Board of Trustees. Thanks to the extraordinary efforts of Louise Brown Farnum, Wellsville became the recipient of a generous donation of $17,600 from Mr. Howe honoring his former hometown to build the original David A. Howe Library on the corner of North Main and Jefferson Streets, which opened in 1910. The Library's success quickly led to the need for more space. Mrs. Brown continued to encourage her nephew to consider additional funding for a new and larger library. David A. Howe left the bulk of his estate, $1,250,000, to bring Mrs. Brown's dream to fruition. David A. Howe did not live to see the opening of the new library because he passed away October 27, 1925 from a stroke. However, the interest income from Mr. Howe's bequest was allowed to accumulate for ten-years providing the necessary funds to build the current structure. The principal of the estate bequest provided sufficient income for the Library to be financially independent for almost half a century.

The structural design of the David A. Howe Public Library is an inviting U-shaped residential Georgian colonial style building of Harvard brick trimmed with Indiana limestone. The roof was shingled with hand-made clay tiles. Flagstone terraces border the front and back of the library. Architect Carl Ade of Rochester, New York designed the structure with building starting in 1935 and ending in 1937. The construction cost

Exterior, original David A. Howe Library (1910-1937)

$340,000 and $25,000 to furnish. The Hayden Company of Rochester, interior design firm, selected reproductions of furniture styles from the reigns of William and Mary and Queen Anne.

The oak ionic columns separate a central hall of rift sawn oak from the Reading and Reference Rooms. A portrait of David A. Howe in a limewood frame hangs behind the front desk. Above each doorway are carvings representing the *Tree of Life*, the *Lamp of Knowledge*, and the *Hive of Industry*. The Reference and Reading Rooms are high ceilinged and spacious with comfortable chairs distributed to encourage browsing and reading. Paneled walls, bookcases, and files characterize the Local History Room, which offers a quiet and more secluded area for research and study. The Exhibition Space has floor to ceiling windows on three sides and is more subdued allowing the displayed items to garner their deserved attention. The Georgian design of the Monday Club Room serves the activities for many community organizations with facilities to offer luncheons. A Portrait of Louise Farnum Brown can be found on the back wall of this room. The Children's Library is painted in more expressive colors to entice young readers to browse low case book shelves, sit in comfortable maple furniture, and enjoy a wood burning fireplace. The Library's Board Room found additional service as a large print room, music room, and microfilm reading room. The Nancy Howe Auditorium is entered from the rear lower level of the three-story structure. The auditorium accommodates 340 people and was designed to offer theatrical productions, host invited lecturers, and serve community gatherings.

1910, Reading Room, original David A. Howe Library

1937, Main Reading Room, David A. Howe Public Library

In 1937 the new David A. Howe Public Library could boast a collection of 9,000 items. Today, the library is the repository of over 110,000 items, which include books, magazines, video and DVD, audio, and electronic resources. Since World War II, the library has been the site of bowling rallies, boating safety classes, automobile shows, author talks, antique appraisals, clogging exhibitions, Miss Allegany County judging pageants, and music concerts. Sadly, the back gardens were the victim of Hurricane Agnes in 1972 when a new flood control project necessitated the Genesee River's diversion and street redesign. Recent library directors have successfully raised funds, which enabled the restoration of the Terrace and the Auditorium. The maintenance of such a distinguished structure is expensive and Wellsville and its residents take great pride in keeping David A. Howe's gift at its splendid best. Louise Farnum Brown did not live to see the new Library's completion, but she was the Library's *mother*. To this day a descendant of Louise Farnum Brown has always served on the David A. Howe Public Library's Board of Trustees.

1937, Exterior, David A. Howe Public Library

1937, Reference Room, David A. Howe Public Library

1937, View through Reference Room to the Monday Club Room, David A. Howe Public Library

1937, Monday Club Room, David A. Howe Public Library

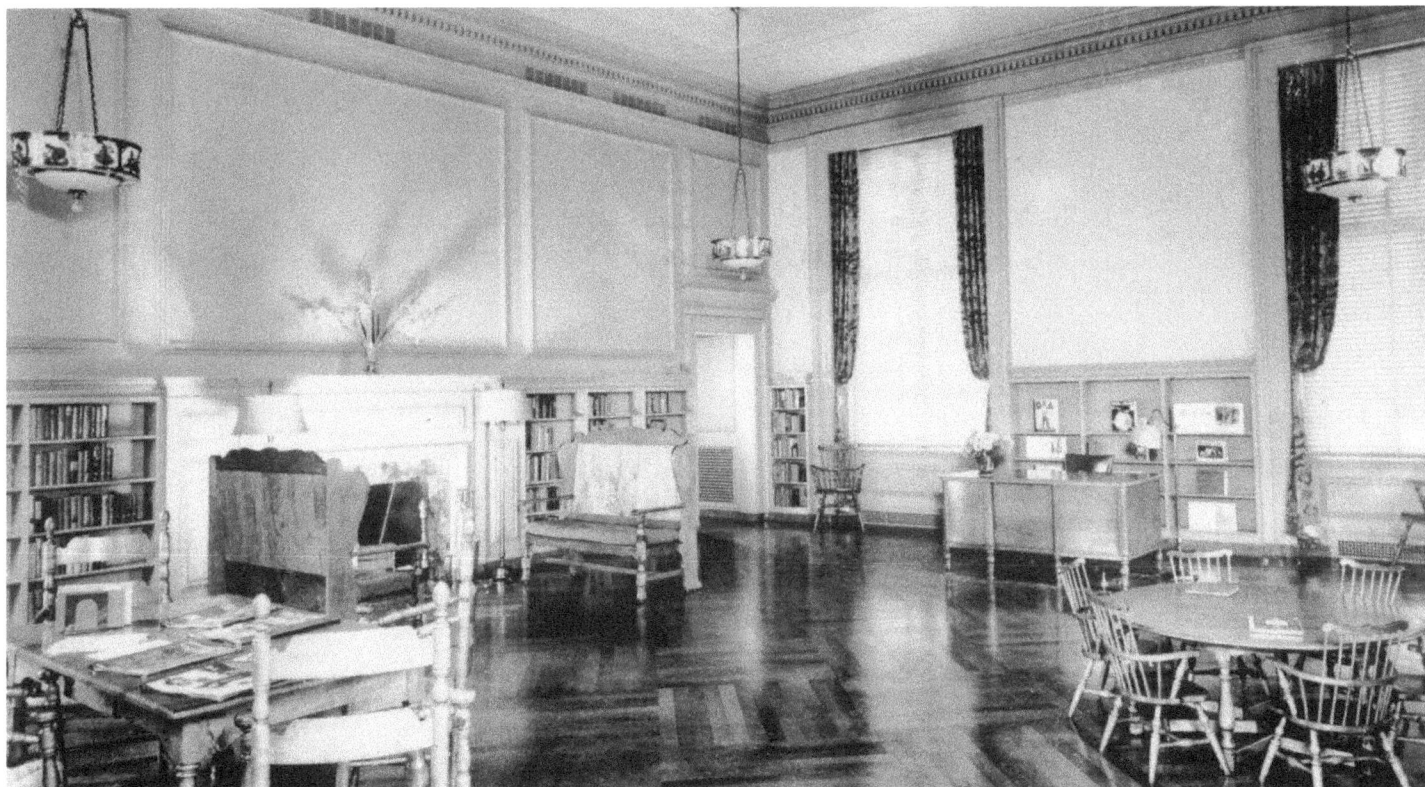

1937, Children's Reading Room, David A. Howe Public Library

143

1937, Nancy Howe Auditorium, David A. Howe Public Library

1937, Terrace, David A. Howe Public Library

1937, Auditorium Entrance and Gardens, David A. Howe Public Library

APPENDIX
Photo Credits

A special thank you goes to Mike C. Beaty for the days and weeks of time he devoted to scanning and professionally touching up hundreds of old photographs to enable the best selection of images for use in this book.

Dust Jacket Front: Woelfel Archives
Dust Jack Back: Woelfel Archives

Unless otherwise stated below all the photographs in this publication are from the family archives of the *Hall-Carpenter-Woelfel* family.

Paquette Archives:

- Chapter 1: images 13, 14, 15, 16, 17, and 18.
- Chapter 3: images 5, 6, and 7.
- Chapter 4: images 14, 17, 18, 19, 20, 26, and 27.
- Chapter 6: images 4, 5, and 14.
- Chapter 7: images 1 and 4.
- Chapter 10: images 8-10.
- Chapter 11: images: 1-13.

Open Source:

- Chapter 2: image of P. T. Barnum.
- Chapter 3: image of Hanford Gordon Lennox

Bridgeport, Connecticut Historical Society:

- Chapter 4: image of Eli Thompson residence.

Library of Congress:

- Chapter 4: image of 1907 Wellsville, N. Y. Sanford Insurance Map.

SELECTED BIBLIOGRAPHY

Beers, F. W. *History of Allegany County, New York, 1806-1879.* NY: F. W. Beers & Co., 1879.

Bogan, Robert V. *Images of America: Angelica, Belmont, and Wellsville.* Dover, New Hampshire: Arcadia Press, 1998.

Brilvitch, Charles. Retired Bridgeport, Connecticut City Historian for his research on the Hall Family and the documentation on the Eli Thompson residence.

Doty, Lockwood R., ed. *History of Genesee Country.* Chicago, IL: S. J. Clarke Publishing Co., 1925, 4 Volumes.

Doty, William Joseph, ed. *The Historic Annals of Southwestern New York, 1940.* NY: Lewis Historical Publishing Co., Inc., 1940. 3 Volumes.

Gillon, Edmund V., Jr. and Clay Lancaster. *Victorian Houses: A Treasury of Lesser-Known Examples.* NY: Dover Publications, 1973. Plate/Page 36 has a black and white photograph of the Pink House along with a brief narrative.

Hernick, Linda VanAller. "Edwin Bradford Hall: Devonian Sponge Collector *Extraordinaire,*" *Earth Sciences History*, v. 22, no. 2, 2003, pp. 209-218.

Hetzel, Tracy. *W(Ella's)Ville.* Baltimore, MD: J.H. Hurst Printing, Inc., 2013, 2nd Ed. Narrative on Wellsville, including Mr. Hall and the Pink House.

Jones, Louis C. *Things That Go Bump in the Night.* NY: Hill and Wang, 1959. A very inaccurate story about the Pink House is related on pages 112-16.

Maass, John. *The Victorian Home in America.* NY: Hawthorn Books, 1972. Color Plate VI and page 78 contains a brief narrative and a black and white photograph on the Pink House. The Pink House is pictured on the book's dust jacket.

Minard, John S. *Allegany County and its People.* Alfred, NY: W. A. Fergusson and Co., 1896.

Naversen, Kenneth. *East Coast Victorians.* Wilsonville, OR: Beautiful America Publishing Co., 1990. Pages 76-77 offer a brief narrative and a photograph on the Pink House.

Pomada, Elizabeth and Michael Larsen. *America's Painted Ladies.* NY: Dutton Studio Books, 1992. Three photographs and a brief narrative on the Pink House pages 57-60.

Smith, A. G. *Victorian Houses, A Dover Coloring Book.* Mineola, NY: Dover Publications, Inc., 2001. Image 8 for coloring is the Pink House.

Thelma Rogers Genealogical and Historical Society. *Images of America: Wellsville.* Charleston, South Carolina: Arcadia Press, 2015.

Wellsville Daily Reporter, Wellsville, New York. Selected Issues.

ABOUT THE AUTHORS

Dr. **Julian Bradford Woelfel** was the great-grandson of Edwin Bradford Hall. He inherited the *Pink House* along with his brother, Bruce Woelfel, upon the death of his grandmother, Fannie Hall Carpenter in 1958. Dr. Woelfel purchased his brother's interest in the *Pink House* becoming the residence's sole owner along with his wife, Marcile. Julian Woelfel was a *Professor Emeritus* of the College of Dentistry Prosthodontics Department of Ohio State University in Columbus, Ohio. Julian came to Columbus from New York City when he was twelve years of age when his father accepted a faculty position in the College of Education at Ohio State University. Julian Woelfel attended the University School on the campus, graduated in 1943, and enrolled in the Ohio State University Pre-Dent Navy V-12 program, graduating in March 1948. Dr. Julian Woelfel joined the Ohio State University Dental Faculty with the rank of dental intern. Dr. Woelfel taught, did research, attended professional society meetings, and lectured in eighteen foreign countries including Wales, Ireland, Turkey, Bulgaria, and Romania. In 1967 Julian was a *Visiting Professor* in Nihon University, Tokyo, Japan for four months. After retiring in 1989, Dr. Woelfel was again a *Visiting Professor* for three months in Taiwan and Brazil and for six months in London, England. The ninth edition of his textbook, *Dental Anatomy*, was published in 2017 and remains widely used in Dental Schools in both the United States and Abroad. Julian held two dental patents, which he gave to Ohio State University. For two years, Dr. Julian Woelfel was a Research Associate at the National Bureau of Standards in Washington, D. C. He made dentures using many different materials to be eligible for certification in the United States. Dr. Woelfel was a veteran of the Korean War and was a Captain in the United States 1st Armored Division at Fort Hood, Texas. He managed the Army Dental Laboratory there for two years. In retirement, he and his wife, Marcile, visited and toured extensively China, South America, Costa Rica, many South Pacific Islands, Europe, Africa, Madagascar with two exciting journeys to Easter Island and Papua New Guinea. Dr. Julian Woelfel died unexpectedly on September 2, 2017 at 91 years, four months shy of his 92nd birthday.

Marcile B. Woelfel was born in Defiance County in northeastern Ohio where she graduated from high school. Marcile received a scholarship to attend Capital University in Bexley, Ohio, a suburb of Columbus. Marcile met her future husband, Julian Woelfel, when she was a student at Capital when her college roommate decided to go to the Jimmy Rawlins Dance School in downtown Columbus during the summer. Julian and a friend decided to take dance lessons there as well. Julian had an old coupe car and began taking Marcile home after dance class. They dated for two years while Julian finished dental school. Julian and Marcile were married May 1, 1948 and settled near Ohio State University. Julian and Marcile raised three sons. Bradford Woelfel, the eldest, is a graduate of Ohio State University High School, Oberlin College (B. A.), Ohio State University School of Education (M. A.), and Capital University Law School. Brad worked in Juvenile Court until his retirement. Brad and his wife, Margo, have been married for thirty years and reside in Columbus. The Woelfel's second son, Barry Edwin, attended the New College in Sarasota, Florida and Ohio State University before moving to California where he graduated from Sonoma College. Barry received a degree in library science from Berkeley University. Julian's and Marcile's youngest son, Jay Bryan, graduated from the Ohio State University Department of Cinema and Film and moved to Los Angeles area in California. Jay has been actively involved in the film industry making his own movies and doing sound for other films. Jay and his wife, Kristy, a former Ohio resident, currently reside in Glendale. After the Woelfel family returned from Japan in 1967, Marcile was invited by the Ohio State University Director of Foreign Affairs to become involved in a new program at the university for the wives and children of foreign students. Ohio State University was experiencing a rapid increase in foreign students studying for advanced degrees. An International Wives Club was formed to program classes in English, pregnancy, child care, grocery shopping, and many more to assist in assisting the foreign students and their families'

adjustment to adjusting to American culture and life-style. Meetings were frequently organized at nearby churches. Marcile Woelfel was the volunteer chairperson for this program for twenty years ending with Julian's 1989 retirement. The International Wives Club was eventually phased out as more spouses of foreign students preferred to enroll in regular academic courses at Ohio State University. In addition to their extensive international travel in retirement, Julian and Marcile began the extensive restoration of the *Pink House* in Wellsville, New York. Marcile celebrated her 91st birthday January 24, 2018.

William A. Paquette, Ph. D. (United States) was a Professor of History at Tidewater Community College in Portsmouth, Virginia where he taught Latin American History, World Civilization, U. S. History, and Western Civilization. Professor Paquette received a Master's Degree from Duquesne University (Pittsburgh) and a Ph. D. from Emory University (Atlanta). During his academic career, Dr. Paquette was awarded 14 National Endowment for the Humanities Grants for professional study and Institutional grants that enabled him to study and conduct research in China and Japan. He traveled to southern Mexico over a ten-year period examining the archaeology at Maya and Aztec sites and studied the Maya language at Duke University (Durham, NC). Professor Paquette presented research at international conferences at the University of Louvain (Belgium), the Sorbonne (Paris), the University of Acala de Henares (Spain), the University of Copenhagen (Denmark), Lorand Eotvos University (Budapest), and San Pablo University (Madrid). He has published over 165 articles and nine books and served as a consultant to the U.S. Department of Education, the United States Institute of Peace, the National Endowment for the Humanities, and all major history textbook publishers. For a decade, he was the History Editor for the international MERLOT (Multimedia Education Resources for Learning and Online Teaching) Project instructing college and university faculty on how to teach online courses. In 2016, Dr. Paquette went to Eastern Europe to study firsthand the legacy of World War II and Communism on the people and nations of Bulgaria, Romania, Serbia, Hungary, Slovakia, Austria, and the Czech Republic.

During his professional career Dr. Paquette met the late King Michael I and the late Queen Anne of Romania, King Simeon II of Bulgaria, the late Pope John Paul II, the Dalai Lama, members of the British Royal Family, and numerous Heads of Government from European States. Dr. Paquette resided for ten years in Wellsville, New York where he attended Wellsville's High School, one block away from Edwin B. Hall's fabled *Pink House*.

Dr. Jullian and Marciole Woelfel are the current owners of The Pink House. Dr. Woelfel is the great-grandson of Edwon Bradford Hall.

www.ingramcontent.com/pod-product-compliance
Lightning Source LLC
Chambersburg PA
CBHW042353030426
42336CB00029B/3466